FARMERS

IN PREHISTORIC BRITAIN

FARMERS

IN PREHISTORIC BRITAIN

Francis Pryor

TEMPUS

To three highly charged individuals:
Richard Rigg, Garner Roberts and Bill Watson

First published 1998

Published by:
Tempus Publishing Limited
The Mill, Brimscombe Port
Stroud, Gloucestershire, GL5 2QG

Typesetting and origination by Tempus Publishing Ltd.
Printed and bound in Great Britain.

British Library Cataloguing in Publication Data.
A catalogue record for this book is available from the British Library.

ISBN 07524 1403 8

Contents

The illustrations

Cover

Soay sheep of the darker strain grazing at the Bronze Age farm at Flag Fen, Peterborough. Primitive sheep of this type would have been found in their thousands in Fenland pastures from about 1800 BC.

Text illustrations

Colour plates

(between pages 64 and 65)

Acknowledgements

Books are written best when one feels relaxed with the world. Since moving to the Lincolnshire Fens I have felt very much at ease and I will always have a very soft spot for the archaeologists and others who have made me so welcome to their county.

Turning next to the practical business of writing a book, first and foremost I must acknowledge the help I have received from my wife, Maisie. The book was written over two lambing periods, and there were numerous occasions when I ought to have been in the lambing pens, acting the part of her obstetrical assistant, but was actually to be found indoors, in the warm — and at the word-processor. I have had very fruitful discussions about Bronze Age fields with David Coombs, Richard Bradley, Chris Chippindale, Charles French, Steve Catney, Chris Evans and David Knight, and owe a special debt of gratitude to Tom Lane, with whom I worked, very happily, on the Welland Bank project. Tom's organisation (Archaeological Project Services) very kindly prepared much of the artwork, especially the maps and cropmark plots to do with Deeping Bank and other sites in the lower Welland valley. The artist at APS was Dave Hopkins.

The site supervisor at Welland Bank, Mark Dymond, was in every respect a perfect right-hand man and helped make the dig a success. Chris Scurfield kindly sent me a copy of his Trent metalwork paper and Jonathan Hunn has generously given me access to his data on West Deeping. I would also like to acknowledge the help I received from the late Penri Jones, tutor in sheep management at the Cambridgeshire College of Agriculture at Milton. Finally, a very special word of thanks to David Yates who sent me copies of his forthcoming paper in the *Oxford Journal of Archaeology* and extracts from his MA thesis.

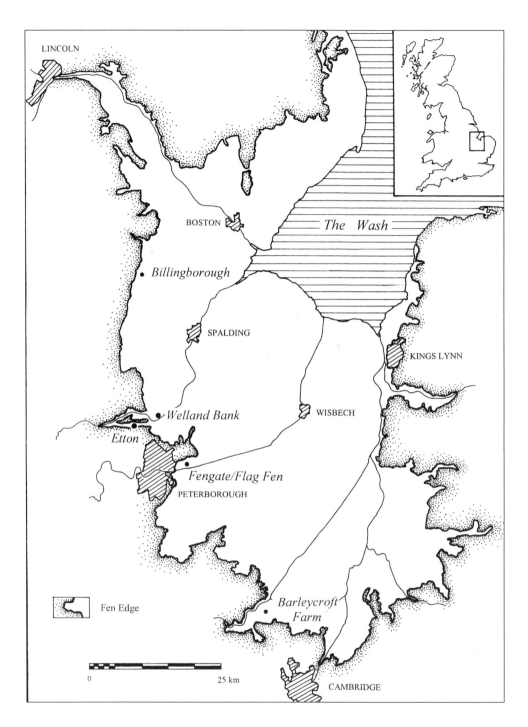

LINCOLN

BOSTON

The Wash

Billingborough

SPALDING

KINGS LYNN

Welland Bank

WISBECH

Etton

Fengate/Flag Fen

PETERBOROUGH

Fen Edge

Barleycroft Farm

0   25 km

CAMBRIDGE

1   *Map, showing the main sites mentioned in the text.*

1 Farmers and prehistory

The main purpose of this book is to discuss the origins and development of a uniquely British style of intensive livestock farming that flourished for about a thousand years during the Bronze Age. It was confined, so far as we know, to lowland areas and there is abundant evidence that, in simple economic terms, it was highly successful.

The recognition and subsequent research into these intensive livestock farming landscapes has been most exciting. Given the pace of archaeological research, it has all happened very fast: mostly in the past 25 years. Unlike much archaeological research in Britain, this particular topic has developed as a result of developer-funded, commercial excavations, which have taken place as a precondition of obtaining Planning Permission. At present the country's urban economy is healthy and, as a result, the momentum of research is steadily increasing.

In most place the episode of intensive livestock farming lasted for about a millennium, spread between the years 1500 and 500 BC. If, however, we are to understand something as complex as a system of farming it will be necessary to take a good long run at it. So I propose to start with the roots of British farming, which lie back in the fifth and sixth millennia BC.

One final word. I have most decidedly *not* written a textbook, as I firmly believe that our knowledge of prehistoric farming is still in its infancy. Textbooks, if they are to have authority, require more hard-and-fast facts than I believe we can muster at this stage.

A personal slant

Now there are as many archaeologies as there are archaeologists. Ours is a subject that pretends to be 'objective', sometimes even 'scientific', but in reality it is a humanity — with all that that implies. As archaeologists we may try to present both sides of every argument, but as human beings we inevitably tip the scales in favour of the views we happen to hold. So the purpose of this chapter is to introduce the reader to the particular set of biases and personal idiosyncrasies that will inform — some would say distort, others, more charitably perhaps, colour — the pages that follow.

I have been fascinated by prehistoric farming since I first realised, way back in 1971, that my excavations had stumbled across an ancient field boundary. The site in question, Fengate, lies on the outskirts of Peterborough, and will feature throughout this book. In the weeks that followed the discovery of that first straight ditch, I combed the literature

2   *Excavating Bronze Age droveway ditches, Fengate 1971. At the time we had no idea of the ditches' original purpose. So we were digging 'blind' — never a wise strategy.*

for a clue to what it might actually have been. I wanted answers and explanations as a matter of extreme urgency, but then I was 25 years old, and the notion of 'everything in its own time' had yet to cross my path.

I had discovered a prehistoric ditch, and I was very excited about it. My team carefully excavated (**2**) the dark grey silt that filled it and we revealed tiny pieces of Bronze Age pottery. So I had discovered a Bronze Age ditch.

The next step was to examine air photos of the area to see whether there were other, perhaps similar ditches in the area — and there were. In fact there were about a dozen of them, often arranged in pairs resembling the side ditches of roads or trackways. But like a good archaeologist I ignored this obvious explanation in my search for a deeper truth.

Hillforts were very big news in archaeological circles in the early '70s, and various scholars were demonstrating that many Iron Age hillforts had their origins way back in the Bronze Age. My ditch — of which I was now inordinately proud — was not, however, in hilly countryside. I should have realised the significance of this when I rashly decided that it and the unexcavated ditches on the air photos formed part of a system of ancient defences-in-depth, analogous to the spectacular hillforts of Wessex. Mercifully for my subsequent reputation I gave vent to this absurd idea in private only. The point I am trying to make is that all archaeologists invest so much time, care, effort and expertise in their research that the results *have* to be exciting. Anything else would be a huge let-down.

14

My ditched defences-in-depth — with their exciting connotations of Boadicean-style chariot warfare and blue-painted warriors — turned out to be nothing more glamorous than a few farm tracks. My disappointment on realising their actual significance was devastating. I can remember it vividly even now. But it then took upwards of a decade for a more profound truth slowly to dawn: that the trackways were actually far more exciting than the supposed defences, because they provided the crucial evidence on the way ancient people organised their land, their livestock — and their lives.

Flatlands and wetlands

My archaeological background and experience is unfashionably parochial. I have spent almost every year of my professional life, since the discovery of those Bronze Age ditches in 1971, working in and around the Fens of East Anglia. I have made short forays abroad — notably to Holland — but never for long. I have always returned to the flatlands around the Wash. Some people would see my perspective as limited, maybe even blinkered, but I would argue that ancient life was so complex that only detailed and long-term study of any given region will begin to reveal how things actually *worked*: how the people earned their living; how they got on with each other; who they considered to be friends, neighbours, rivals, enemies or foreigners.

Superficially the Fenland landscape appears simple. It's flat and wet, or rather it was wet before it was drained. It must be admitted that the modern Fens can be rather dreary, especially in the more intensive arable areas (**3**), but there are still large tracts of countryside where trees and hedges survive and where cattle peacefully graze (**4**).

A wet landscape conceals a myriad of micro-landscapes which only the inhabitants fully understand. Ask someone from the Low Countries how many words there are for water and wet places in Dutch, and you'll be listening for a long time. This richness of language reflects the way people perceive their challenging landscape: it is complex, changing, dangerous even, but never dull. Personally I have found the Fens and the countryside around them enormously challenging. It is difficult archaeology to comprehend and it can be almost as difficult to dig. But by the same token it is very easy indeed to misinterpret, or to jump to the wrong conclusions. In Fenland archaeology, nothing is ever simple. I certainly wouldn't live or work anywhere else.

The archaeologist as farmer

While the archaeology of Fenland has been a major preoccupation of my life so far, I come from a farming family and have always enjoyed nature, wildlife and the countryside. To be a farmer one needs land, and in Britain it is almost impossible to get started in farming unless one inherits a farm. That was not to be my lot — and to be honest I am not sure that I would have welcomed the opportunity, had it arisen. Land ownership is nothing of the sort — one is a steward of any given plot for life only, and one has a duty to hand it on in good condition. It's a huge responsibility. It would also have been very difficult to have farmed professionally and to have been an archaeologist. So I did it the other way around.

In Britain, unlike Germany, France and other European countries, it is still unusual to

3   *The other Fenland: arable fields alongside a main drainage dyke near Whittlesey. Until 1850 this peat land was only good for rough grazing and wildfowl; it lay next to Whittlesey Mere, then the largest body of freshwater in England.*

4   A tranquil Fenland scene: cattle grazing the lush grassland of the river Nene washes near Whittlesey. Note the high level of water in the dyke.

combine farming with other ways of earning an honest crust. Across the EU small farmers are increasingly being forced to leave the land in the face of poor returns on their labour and a horrifying welter of bureaucratic paperwork. One way around the problem is to farm professionally, but part-time. That is the way I have done it. And if you really want to make me annoyed, call me a hobby-farmer.

My way of approaching the problem of how to start in farming was to specialise in much the same way that I had specialised in archaeology. So for various reasons — not the least being expense — I found myself keeping sheep (**5**). It was hard to get started and we borrowed and spent much money on land, fencing and equipment. I know full well that my bank manager would not allow our newly-formed enterprise to become a mere hobby.

Even now, 12 years after we started, our farming partnership *has* to make money — enough to pay myself and my wife, the archaeologist Maisie Taylor, for the six to eight weeks we spend working on the farm each year. This commercial discipline has actually been very useful and informative, and it has helped me understand some of the imperatives behind some of the decisions to adopt specific livestock handling measures in the past. Certainly where livestock are concerned, if one wants to do a job thoroughly there is usually only one way to do it. Often one arrives at that one way after a long and expensive process of trial-and-error.

But of course money alone is not why we both farm sheep: the profit-and-loss accounts make no allowances for the twice daily walk through the flock with Jess the dog, nor do

5   *The joys of spring. Each year we take a photograph of the young lambs as they are turned out to grass for the first time. This is the scene in March 1997. In the foreground is a coloured Shetland ewe with her twin white (x Lleyn) lambs behind her.*

they cost-in the delight at seeing a Marsh Harrier swoop on a hare, and they certainly do not allow for the pleasure we both derive, every hour of every day, just from living deep within the English countryside.

We started farming sheep, but in a very small way indeed, some ten years ago. At the time we had the use of a small paddock whose Fenland soil grew grass too lush for my poor lawnmower to cope with. So we bought four Suffolk x Jacob ewes from the County Archaeologist of Norfolk (an authority on the Norfolk Horn breed), Dr Peter Wade-Martins, who warned us at the time that keeping sheep could become a dangerous obsession. He was absolutely right.

Those four black sheep produced an annual crop of ten or twelve lambs and kept our half-acre paddock in tip-top condition. Our approach was, in hindsight, laid-back in the extreme. In late November we would borrow a friendly old ram from a neighbouring farmer and 21 weeks later, in April, lambs would appear. We made no special provision for lambing and we had very few problems. Soon we had begun to accumulate a solid base of customers who appreciated the wonderful flavour and tenderness of unstressed, grass-fed lamb. And there is *nothing* to beat it. At the same time, Maisie's interest in spinning and woollen textiles was growing and sheep — even black sheep — have to be shorn every year. So the commercial possibilities of our tiny enterprise were becoming difficult to ignore.

So, to cut a long story short, we needed more land and in 1991 we decided to move house to find it. The following year we came across an ideal spot with the right sort of soil, minerals and groundwater table, about ten miles north of our old place. At first we bought a single field, but now we farm about 30 acres of grass, and we buy-in fodder beet and straw for winter forage. It's hardly a big spread, but as I write it supports about 120 breeding ewes and their lambs (say 240 on a very good year). So our stocking rate is about four ewes to the acre, which is fairly conservative. As a matter of interest, more intensive farmers can manage seven or more ewes to the acre with no real difficulty, unless of course the summer is as dry as some recent summers have been. Two years ago (in 1996) I was forced to feed our sheep hay in August to put them into sufficiently good condition for the ram in early October. I have never known a season like it — but then that's the British farmer's perennial moan.

We over-winter our sheep, under cover, from Christmas to April and lamb in March. We keep two breeds: a small flock of about 30 coloured Shetlands and a larger flock of more commercial Lleyns. Shetland sheep are smaller than average and have many primitive characteristics apart from size, but they produce superb fleeces and their meat is also finely textured and of very good flavour, but not as 'gamey' as some very primitive sheep, such as the Soay or mouflon.

Lleyns have their origins in the Lleyn peninsula of north Wales and are currently enjoying something of a revival, from being a rare breed a few years ago. They too have fine fleeces (traditionally used for socks), but they are mainly noted for their extraordinary prolificacy: twins are usual, triplets common and last year we had one set of quins! They are slightly smaller than the usual sheep one sees in lowland England, which are often Suffolk, Texel or Leicester (so-salled 'Mules') crosses, but I want lightweight sheep both because they are easier to handle, and because they do not poach our soft, silty Fen soil in wet weather.

We sell our wool to the Wool Marketing Board and like the wool from most British breeds it goes to make worsteads and carpets. As a matter of interest, most of the fine knitting wool used today comes from Australian Merino sheep; Merinos have their origins in Spain and are not reliably hardy in the cool, Atlantic climate of British Isles. Even the wool of our own Shetland sheep tends to form a felty mat if the animals are not protected from the worst of the winter's rains. The money we get for our wool just about covers the cost of shearing — so things have changed a great deal from Medieval times when wool, of course, was the basis of East Anglia's wealth.

Our meat lambs are sold to local butchers and private customers, but the majority is auctioned at market — usually at Melton Mowbray, since the recent closure of the more local market at King's Lynn. Markets are — and always have been — important to country people as a place to do business and to meet old friends. I would say that the social side of markets is probably of slightly more importance (although they would never admit it!) to most farmers than the business of buying and selling. There is, however, a perception in certain urban circles that markets are somehow wrong and that they should be closed down. I do hope the well-intentioned people who propound such views will one day realise what they are doing, and the effect their words could have on rural life. It would appear that they think that the world would be a more humane place if livestock were bought and sold on the Internet. Maybe, but we should consider the welfare of humans too. Compassion for world farmers, perhaps.

This brings me to the unavoidable topic of meat and death. I say unavoidable, because in the past — even the recent past — the connection was obvious: the butcher's shop contained whole or half carcasses which were displayed, usually both indoors and in the street, with pride. Today most households buy their meat in neatly wrapped supermarket packages and the connection between a living beast and the food it provides can be — and is — side-stepped. In many ways supermarket meat, eggs, dairy products and other animal-derived foods have become 'virtual foods' — in the sense of 'virtual reality'. They are as devoid of any connection with the countryside, as they are tasteless. Accordingly, farming and animal husbandry have become dissociated from food in many people's minds. This in turn removes the causal and emotional link between consumer and supplier. That at least is my explanation for why urban society has become so antipathetic towards the people who actually feed them.

If I have lambs to be slaughtered I like to see them into the slaughterhouse myself. In the past I have seen them dispatched, but today hygiene regulations prevent this. I by no means enjoy the process of slaughter, I have never met a farmer who does, but afterwards there is a sense of having completed a job well: the animals died unstressed and they were in good physical condition. When they were alive they were properly cared-for and lived in a community of other sheep and on good grass. When dead they will provide people with healthy meat. I can say with a clear conscience that I have nothing to apologise for — and I suspect that my Bronze Age forebears thought much the same.

Farmers and farming

I must now say a few words about our subject matter: farmers. First we must be clear about the word itself. I shall use the term in its widest possible sense: farmers were people and communities who produced food from the land, whether by horticulture/arable or by herding and tending livestock. It is harder to define what precisely one means by 'farm*ing*'. Where does one draw the line? We have just discussed markets; now does farming end when the farmer leaves the farm, enters the sale-ring, or the pub at lunchtime?

My own view is that the entire day at market is part of the farming year. But what about when the farmer or his family go to church on Sunday, is that farming? What about Christmas and Harvest Festival? Again, coming from a rural community I would suggest that these too are an integral part of the farming year. So what I will have to write about will be rural life in ancient times, but with a heavy emphasis on food-production.

The time periods will be the Neolithic, Bronze and Iron Ages. Bearing in mind that human prehistory in Britain begins around half a million years ago in the Palaeolithic or Old Stone Age, the epoch we are concerned with can broadly be defined as later prehistory.

Archaeologists tend to partition time to suit their own purposes. So a specialist in the complex development of Romano-British brooches will need to have many more and smaller slices of time to work with, than someone like myself, who paints on a broader canvas and deals with less specific processes, such as social change. I also tend to use a variety of terms to indicate greater or lesser precision. The main point to bear in mind is that the dates which appear in the table are not hard-and-fast: there are no actual fixed moments — such as 1066 — in north European later prehistory, so when I state that the

Bronze/Iron Age transition happened around 600-700 BC, the actual spread of time is probably in the order of 50 years on either side of that century.

The great advantage of regional archaeology is that it allows one to examine processes of change through time — and in considerable detail. It is this, the passage of great spans of time, which makes archaeology's contribution to contemporary knowledge so very important.

Archaeology has benefited enormously from advances made in the study of past environments. Thanks to the detailed scientific work of colleagues like Dr Charles French of Cambridge University, I can now write with some confidence about soils that were, or were not, ploughed. At present, the impact of quality information of this sort cannot be assessed outside local or regional contexts. So my scope will be small — deliberately — but I will try to draw some broader conclusions.

Table of dates and periods

Date	Period	Approximate period	Events and innovations
AD 650			
	Early (or Pagan) Saxon		
AD 410			
	Roman		
AD 43			Roman conquest
	Late Iron Age		Wheel-made pottery
200 BC			Celtic art flourishes
	Middle Iron Age		
400 BC		later Iron Age	
	Early Iron Age		
600 BC		earlier Iron Age	
	Bronze/Iron Age transition		Introduction of iron
700 BC			Emergence of 'Celtic' society
	Late Bronze Age		
1000 BC		later Bronze Age	First hillforts
	Middle Bronze Age		
1400 BC		earlier Bronze Age	Beaker pottery
	Early Bronze Age		Introduction of copper, then bronze
2000 BC		Neolithic/Bronze Age transition	
	Late Neolithic		Stonehenge, Avebury etc
3000 BC		later Neolithic	
	Middle Neolithic		Causewayed enclosures
4000 BC		earlier Neolithic	Passage graves
	Early Neolithic		
5000 BC			Introduction of farming
	Mesolithic		
9000 BC			Hunting and gathering food

In the meantime the momentum of research is, if anything, increasing, as commercial development in lowland Britain gathers pace.

2 Beginnings

Experiment and reconstruction

Before we proceed any further it would be useful if I could paint an impressionistic picture of a prehistoric farm and the best way to do this is by means of experimental archaeology. So the illustrations in this chapter derive from my experiments in recreating ancient fields and structures. They are experiments and not recreations; so their accuracy and authenticity are always open to question. Unlike scientific experiments archaeological experiments cannot be proved right or wrong. The only real proof of an archaeological experiment would be to turn the clock back — and sadly that's impossible.

I used to believe that experimental archaeology — the attempt to recreate life in the past by practical means — can help us rediscover many of the mysteries of ancient life, provided, that is, we don't bite off more than we can chew. I spent two years working in the Work Study Department of a brewery and there I learned that the scientific study of working rates and production targets almost depended on one thing alone: the mental attitude of the people doing the work. So if people were suitably motivated they could achieve the near-impossible. This must have applied to the past, too. It is not for nothing that Stonehenge, for example, was quite recently considered to be the work of giants. And as for Ely cathedral — I still find it hard to believe that it was built by mere mortals who were unable to suspend the laws of gravity.

It follows that, if we know nothing about motivation or the composition of the workforce, then certain questions should not even be attempted. For example, how long did it take to build Stonehenge? For all I know the work was so special that it could only be carried out left-handed, after dark and when intoxicated after prolonged religious feasting and fasting. So I stay clear of the quantitative, 'how long?' or the 'how many people would it have taken?' questions. Instead I use experimentation to gain less tangible, qualitative insights: what was involved in the construction of prehistoric houses? Was it simpler to build turf-roofed (**6,7**) or thatched (**8,9**) roundhouses? How did ancient livestock handling systems work? What is it like to fetch primitive sheep with a dog? What was involved when it came to harvesting the natural resources of the Fens (**10**)? How easy was it to split timber with wedges (**11**)? What is it like to do practical work with ancient tools (**12**).

These are all questions that can be answered to the satisfaction of the experimenter. But it's very much harder to communicate one's findings to other people. Maybe that is why I increasingly find that even this qualitative style of experimental archaeology can be

6   *Construction of the wood and timber framework of an earlier Bronze Age farmhouse nearing
completion. The woven hazel wattle walls are immensely strong. This house was unaffected by
the great hurricane of October 1989.*

7   *The earlier Bronze Age farmhouse completed. Note the turf roof is beginning to show signs of
parching in the late spring heat. We tried to keep it green using sprinklers, but were forced to
give this up during a hosepipe ban. To our surprise the grasses on the roof responded to the new
conditions: moisture-loving species were replaced by short-lived annuals (such as meadowgrass)
and more drought tolerant types.*

8   *Many roundhouses were roofed with reed or straw thatch which requires a steeper-pitched roof than the turf-roofed houses. Here we are building an Iron Age farmhouse of a type in use at the Cat's Water settlement, Fengate around 250 BC. We used rope to lash the rafters together, but the evidence for this practice is poor. It is possible that pegs or a more rigid carpenter's solution was found to the problem. Iron nails were not used at this period (so far as we know).*

9   *Lashing the purlins to the main rafters of the Cat's Water Iron Age farmhouse. The steep (45°) pitch of the roof is clearly visible.*

10   *Many early farmers performed tasks that would have been familiar to their hunter-gatherer predecessors and contemporaries. Here Richard Darrah gathers the leaves of the razor-sharp saw-toothed sedge from a Suffolk fen to make a cap to go on the apex of a reconstructed roundhouse.*

11   *Controlled splitting, using seasoned oak wedges. Split newly-felled wood would have been used for a number of tasks around the prehistoric farm, including domestic buildings, barns, fences and stock pens. Splitting or cleaving was the main technique for reducing large timbers until the introduction of heavy-duty saws in Roman times.*

12   *As time progressed tools became more specialised. Here I am using a steel adze to reduce the thickness of an Iron Age roundhouse door lintel. In the Bronze Age an axehead, probably hafted adze-fashion would most likely have been used.*

unsatisfactory, and at worst it can become frankly self-indulgent. I remain to be convinced that such direct routes to the past are necessarily reliable. But they can be great fun.

European origins — a revolution?

The actual origins of farming will never be pinned-down accurately, just as one will never be able to say who precisely invented the wheel. In both instances the answer is that different people came across, or were inspired to have, the ideas at different times. From our point of view what matters is that the ideas happened — and were accepted.

The earliest evidence for farming in Europe is found at a number of sites in the extreme south-east, in Greece, Macedonia and the Balkans. The earliest of these sites can be dated by radiocarbon to about 6000 BC. Sites a millennium or more earlier are found in Turkey and farther afield in the Near East and it has generally been assumed that farming was 'invented' in these areas and then spread into Europe. But there are now good reasons to doubt whether in fact this happened, and it is entirely possible that the ideas behind farming were independently arrived-at by the European communities living west of the Black Sea. I do not think it really matters which school of thought is right. The important point is that people and populations in the area were ready to adopt the new ideas. By and large inventions only catch-on if society is ready to accept them — Leonardo da Vinci may have been the first to think of the helicopter, but he certainly did not invent or fly one — and that, as I have already said, is all that matters.

The early prehistory of southern and eastern European farming does seem to mark a fairly profound break from the previous, hunter-gatherer, way of life. Closer to Britain, around the North Sea basin, the distinction, as we will see, is far less clear-cut. The introduction of farming is considered to be the main distinguishing aspect of the Neolithic or New Stone Age. And the Neolithic marked a major change from the Mesolithic which preceded it — or so conventional wisdom would have us believe.

With farming went a number of new developments and inventions, including permanent houses, village-like communities, the first pottery (and with it the greater use and control of fire), polished as opposed to chipped stone technology and many other smaller innovations. These mainly technological changes affected contemporary societies so profoundly that many archaeologists referred to a 'Neolithic Revolution' on the lines of the Industrial Revolution. In fact I can remember writing a (very poor) critique of the idea for my degree exams.

Now when the idea of the Neolithic Revolution was first put forward it attracted a great deal of informed support, but within a few years the first radiocarbon dates began to arrive and it soon became clear that the 'revolution' must have taken at least a thousand years to happen. As revolutions went, it was therefore on the protracted side of instantaneous.

Even today in post-'Neolithic Revolution' times, prehistorians stress the very important social changes that had to accompany the introduction of farming. Once farming had started it became necessary, for example, to live in permanent houses in order to tend the crops and then to guard food reserves over winter. Also, with a more settled lifestyle people were able to work on technologies that could not easily be developed by a community always on the move; of these, the construction of ovens, leading to kilns and the control of heat and fire, was by far the most important. It was the growth of pyrotechnology, which accompanied the firing of pottery, and which developed in the Neolithic, that ultimately lay behind the subsequent Ages of metal.

By way of contrast — indeed stark contrast — communities that survived by hunting and gathering tended to be smaller and lived together in groups or bands. It was thought that hunter-gatherers had an impoverished way of life, compared to their Neolithic successors within their large houses and secure villages, but numerous studies of existing hunter-gatherer societies, from as far afield as the salmon-fishing communities of western Canada to the Bushmen of the Kalahari Desert and the Aboriginies of Australia, have demonstrated that the way of life was far from impoverished. In fact the opposite was true: hunter-gatherers had more time to develop a rich cultural and ideological world; they were not chained slavishly to the land in the way that farmers have always been. Furthermore, although their houses and settlements were sometimes less permanent or elaborately constructed than those of their farmer equivalents, that was not always the case — as the superb log-built houses and villages of, for example, the Pacific salmon-fishing communities so clearly demonstrated. There was nothing inherent in the hunter-gather way of life that necessitated small groups and impoverished dwellings.

The two biggest differences between hunter-gatherer and farming communities were supposed to be about communal territoriality and the control of the means of food-production. Put in English, communal territoriality means that a community in Neolithic times was supposed to have a clear idea about the size and limits of the area it controlled.

This shared knowledge about the territory that a particular community occupied was expressed on the ground in a variety of ways: by the positioning of large earthwork communal tombs, or barrows, near the edges of the territory and by the placing of major social centres near the middle.

Within each communal territory the landscape was probably further sub-divided into the separate holdings of different clans or families. By and large the physical markers of the various Neolithic territories and sub-territories were substantial earthworks that have survived the passage of time well. In other words our Neolithic forebears have left us plenty to work with: we will be able to play around with the interpretation of barrow distribution maps, for many years to come.

Hunter-gatherer communities affect the look and shape of the landscape less than farmers: by and large they cut down fewer trees and do not construct fields, hedges or drystone walls. But this does not mean that they do not understand how the landscape around them is divided-up. Again, work with modern hunter-gatherers has shown that the different groups had a very clear knowledge of their own community's territorial limits. It is just that they chose to mark these boundaries in a more subtle fashion — perhaps by painting a tree or by carving an emblem on a rock. Being more mobile than farmers, their territories had a seasonal element to them, too. Thus the summer hunting ground of group A might also be the winter fishing area for group B. It is not impossible that there were several overlapping chronological or seasonal territories within the same geographical landscape.

Being thinly spread across the landscape, the various hunter-gatherer bands must have been aware of quite distant family ties. Regular meetings must have taken place both to avoid in-breeding and simply to do those things — such as find partners and catch-up with friends and family — that all societies traditionally do during the plentiful months of the year, when 'all is safely gathered in'. There are no reasons to suppose that communication between the various hunter-gatherer bands, out in the woods and lakes, were necessarily any worse or less regular in the Mesolithic than in the subsequent Neolithic period.

The means of production

So much for communal territoriality — but what about the control of the means of food-production, supposedly *the* defining condition of the farming economy? I used to find it instructive that the Ministry that was once in control of food production and distribution in Britain was the Ministry of Agriculture, Fisheries and Food. Both hunting (*ie* fishing) and farming were neatly combined within the same Whitehall department.

But in reality do farmers necessarily control the means of food production any more than their hunter-gatherer equivalents? I think that is very open to question. Neither group can control the climate and, while hunters and fishers do not plant their 'crops', they soon learn to husband the available resources — or starve. I fail to see why the management and husbandry of a natural resource can be seen to differ so markedly from farming — a means of production that theoretically 'controls' the sources of supply.

It used to be thought that hunters did little to affect the occurrence or abundance of their quarry, but recent archaeological and ethnological research has shown that this is not the case. Hunters made numerous clearings in the forest to encourage the growth of succulent shrubs, grass and other non-woody plants. Animals came to these clearings, which were often placed near watering places, and the hunters could take what they pleased, *when* they pleased; in other words, by carrying out certain not very radical management measures, hunters could attract their prey to a spot convenient for them. Again, it is hard to discern a major divide between, say, hunters around an artificial clearing waiting for animals to arrive, and livestock farmers around a market, waiting for animals to be driven in. It's also perfectly possible, indeed probable, that hunters did in fact drive animals into the clearings they had prepared. Either way, who is demonstrating the greater control of the means of production?

The genuinely big difference between the two ways of living undoubtedly lies in the number of people that can be supported on any given area of land. The 'carrying capacity' of farmed land is *vastly* greater than most land that is traditionally hunted or fished.

Good news travels fast

The spread of farming across Europe has been well documented by excavation and radiocarbon dating. At present it would appear that farming reached the north and west extremities of the continent by two distinct routes, or groups of routes: overland by way of the Danube and Rhine valleys to modern Germany, northern France and the Low Countries; or via the Mediterranean to the Alps, or up the Rhone into central and northern France or, finally, across south-western France via the Carcasonne-Narbonne 'gap'. Within these main routeways there were subsidiary cycles or wheels-within-wheels, such as the mountain-to-plain cycle of the Italian/Austrian Dolomites, illustrated so vividly by the discovery recently of the Alpine Iceman.

Archaeologists are still not agreed on the mechanisms behind the spread of farming across Europe. Was it an 'idea' or concept that passed from community to community along existing lines of communication, by word of mouth? If that is the case, then the actual spread, or diffusion of the idea, which took the best part of two thousand years to complete, was very slow indeed. Was the new way of life introduced by migrating tribes — perhaps the Neolithic equivalents of modern gypsies? Again, the process seems to have taken too long to complete by this method and, besides, it is far from certain that the pre-existing indigenous hunter-gatherer communities would necessarily have welcomed the presence of such newcomers.

There will probably be many new theories to account for the spread of farming though Europe, but so far perhaps the most convincing is the so-called 'wave of advance' model first put forward by the Italian geneticist Luigi Cavalli-Sforza and the American archaeologist Albert Ammerman in 1973. The theory is convincing because it is not just based on archaeological speculation, but follows independently-derived principles of population growth and expansion. In essence the model accounts for the spread of farming in terms of population rise and soil exhaustion which together led to short-distance movements of people away from individual farms; in many ways it is also a common-sense concept which takes account of the natural growth of families and the establishment of new farms or the upgrading of old farms which have fallen into disrepair through neglect — processes which continue to this day.

The 'wave of advance' model of agricultural expansion would envisage the formation of new farms every generation and a very approximate average 'wave of advance' across Europe of about 11 miles (18km) for each generation of 25 years. This figure would accord well with the archaeological evidence. Indeed, the model has much to recommend it. As the 'wave of advance' made its slow way across the plains of lowland Europe, the farming communities would undoubtedly have brought in new blood from the population round about, but at the same time they seem to have retained a strong cultural identity of their own.

It is also probable that the 'wave of advance' farmers spoke the same basic language or group of languages. Professor Colin Renfrew has suggested that this language was none other than the Indo-European ancestor of the principal tongues of modern Europe. Some historical linguists vigorously contest this view, but from an archaeological perspective it is very hard to think when else the basic stock of words underlying our languages could have arrived. It is also very hard to come up with a pan-European social development of remotely the same significance as the introduction of farming.

So much for general trends and developments. I won't say that the picture is simple, because it manifestly is not, but it is coherent and it seems to make sense. There is however a slight snag. The distinctive pottery made by the 'wave of advance' farmers is not found in Britain. Does this mean that farming did not reach these islands until very much later? On the whole, I think not. What it might mean is that the 'wave of advance' was breaking-up on the shores of the North Sea: after centuries of relatively smooth progress across the huge distances of the European land-mass, the wave was about to rebound from the edges — like the ripples from a pebble when they reach the sides of a pond.

Early farming around the North Sea basin

The very first farmers of the initial 'wave of advance' seem to have practised mixed farming — *ie* livestock and cereals — and their settlements were mainly confined along the sides of lowland river valleys in Central Europe. With so strong an identity they could have married outside their own communities into local hunter-gatherer societies, but I suspect they would have done so on their own terms — with outsiders coming into the farmsteads, rather than *vice versa*. It is equally possible, of course, that they disallowed such conduct and that they stayed aloof from the local inhabitants in any given area. However, to have remained isolated for upwards of 80 generations, would have been to invite a genetic time-bomb. New blood, via exogamy (marriage outside the community), must surely have been essential.

Towards the fringes of the continent where the wide and flat valleys so beloved of the main 'wave of advance' were becoming fewer and farther between, the impetus and momentum behind the seeming relentless advance began to break down. The new landscapes were smaller-scale and more diverse than the great European plain. The rivers were faster-moving and there were complications: peat bogs, fens, moors, hills and uplands. These were also areas where the indigenous hunter-gatherer communities were particularly successful and well-adapted. The lakes, islands and coastal waters around the southern North Sea basin and up into Denmark and Scandinavia were populated with hunter-fishing communities who evidently made a good living from the waters and shores. Certainly the archaeological evidence for their way of life is extremely rich and exciting: waterlogged sites of these hunter-fishing groups in Denmark have left us carefully arranged cemeteries, finely made canoe-like boats with beautifully carved and decorated paddles. At Star Carr in east Yorkshire there is evidence for domesticated dog at least three thousand years before the first traces of farming could have reached Britain.

These communities may not have 'controlled' their means of livelihood in the farming sense we discussed earlier, but they came very close to it. Do the Lapps 'farm' the reindeer they so closely depend on? One could argue the case either way, I believe. By the same token the communities around the southern North Sea basin lived what one might term a 'climax' hunter-fisher lifestyle: they were extremely well adapted to both the way of life and the environment, and were able to manage the animal resources they depended upon with great skill. It has always been said that the Star Carr dog was a hunter's companion — the equivalent, perhaps, of a gun dog. But it could equally have been used to herd and round-up semi-wild herbivorous animals, just like a modern sheepdog (which will turn its attention to cattle or deer if required to do so).

Although we still lack sufficient Mesolithic sites in Britain to make such a statement with any assurance, I will suggest that in Britain — and certainly in parts of Holland, Germany and Denmark — the carrying capacity of the landscape inhabited by indigenous hunter-fishing communities was quite high. In other words, the environment contained a lot of readily available protein, in the form of fish, fowl and larger animals. This in turn meant that, if the farming 'wave of advance' was to continue on its way unchecked, a considerable number of people would have to remove themselves from the scene. Moreover the fertile loess (an easily tilled wind-borne soil) and terrace gravel valley land of Central Europe had been replaced by wetter landscapes where areas suitable for arable farming were fewer. In these areas the progress of the once relentless 'wave of advance' was far more piecemeal, and contacts with the native hunter-fisher communities were correspondingly closer.

I am not suggesting that the early years of farming around the fringes of continental Europe saw any sudden or drastic deviations from patterns already established for upward of two millennia. Instead certain practices that were already in existence — such as the ability to marry and form alliances outside the farming community — increased in significance. I am also suggesting that the 'mix' of farming practised in these more marginal areas altered significantly. The wetter and hillier landscapes simply would not have been suited to the regular and reliable harvesting of cereal crops.

We know that cereal crops were processed (*ie* were theshed and/or ground into flour) in many places that might otherwise be considered unsuitable (especially in parts of Holland), and in some instances they were probably grown there too. But this does seem to fly in the face of common-sense — like growing tomatoes in Iceland. Could it be possible that the crops in these areas were grown for their own sake, rather than for food alone? In other words, perhaps they were grown simply because they were symbols of the new, Neolithic, way of life — as were the items needed to store and process the grain.

The wetter, more maritime climates of northern Europe are better suited to the husbandry of animals than to the cultivation of cereals on any scale. Nowhere is this more true than in the British Isles. In Ireland the climate is too wet even to grow sheep well — the fleeces tend to felt and the poor animals suffer from liver fluke, foot-rot and a huge variety of other complaints. I know this from painful personal experience of my mother's family's farm in County Wexford. Sheep, especially the shorter-fleeced primitive breeds, could have been, and indeed were, kept, but not, I suspect, in very great numbers (primitive breeds also have the advantage of less rot-prone feet). The traditional animal of the Irish farm is, of course, the cow which is far more tolerant of the wet. And what magnificent milk and butter the cows of Ireland produce!

The slightly drier climate of mainland Britain makes it excellently adapted for sheep and cattle. Nowadays livestock are mainly confined to the western side of the country, where the rainfall is higher, but in the recent past, before wartime 'Dig for Victory', European Community grants and other subsidies had distorted the natural picture out of all recognition, most farms along the eastern side of the country boasted enormous herds of cattle and flocks of sheep. It was East Anglia and Lincolnshire that grew the wool that formed the basis of the hugely lucrative Medieval wool trade to the Low Countries. Even today, Britain is by far and away the largest provider of sheepmeat in the European Community.

So, to sum up, a variety of environmental and human factors, including climate, land-form and natural drainage, plus a large pre-existing and well-adapted population of hunter-fishing groups, combined together radically to alter the 'wave of advance' of farming in continental Europe. Thereafter, in the British Isles and around the southern North Sea and Baltic basins, the spread of farming would be piecemeal and would depend very much on local circumstances. The make-up or composition of the farming 'mix' would differ from one region to another, depending on local growing conditions, ground drainage, micro-climate and, perhaps most significantly of all, on the size, culture and traditions of the pre-existing, 'native' hunter-fisher communities.

Who were the first farmers in Britain?

Who were the first farmers in this fringe area around the southern North Sea basin? I think this is a question that science-based archaeology will be able to answer within the next two decades, using more precise information based on studies of DNA. In the meantime it is almost certainly rash to speculate, but I will do so none the less!

The composition of 'new' versus 'indigenous' blood in a 'wave of advance' community could be forecast using the original figures and formulae provided by Ammerman and Cavalli-Sforza. No model can predict precisely what proportion of new blood was introduced from the indigenous communities — it can only predict minimum levels that would be required to maintain genetic stability. My own feeling is that inter-marriage with local communities probably increased through time and that when the 'wave of advance' came up against the fringes of the North Sea basin the actual genetic composition of the Neolithic communities was closely similar to that of the people living round about. That is not to say, of course, that the cultures of the two groups would have been similar. Quite the reverse, in fact.

I suspect that the first farmers in Britain were relations of the indigenous hunter-gatherers, from the other side of the Channel or the North Sea. Thereafter the physical relationship between the two would have grown closer. I find it ironic that farming was introduced to Britain by the perhaps quite close relatives of the 'native' hunter-gatherers themselves. Maybe, as we will see shortly, that was why they were so keen to emphasise and symbolically express the uniquely Neolithic character of the new way of life. Viewed from an outsider's perspective, it is often small differences between two groups living in the same area that cause the greatest friction; these differences must be expressed, emphasised, rehearsed and re-rehearsed on a regular and recurrent basis. There is something horribly relentless about the process, but eventually — and it may take several centuries — the tensions will resolve themselves. We see something similar happening in Northern Ireland today, and I believe we also could have seen it in earlier Neolithic Britain, some six thousand years ago.

3 Them and Us — expressions of identity

Territorial imperatives

Hardly a week goes by but, idly thumbing through my copy of *Farmers Weekly,* I do not come across a story to do with access. Nine times out of ten it is the Ramblers versus Farmers dispute (usually treated in a very balanced way, I might add), but sometimes it is about the practical problems of farming on the edges of large cities: gates left open, litter, rotten picnic food, vandalism, burnt-out cars, dogs running wild etc, etc.

What lies at the root of these problems? Is it general bloody-mindedness and hostility on both sides, or is it ignorance — also on both sides? Or is it something altogether more profound, to do with the relationship of human beings to land?

When I first started to keep primitive farm livestock at Flag Fen we lost 90% of our small flock of Soay sheep to an attack by two large guard dogs that had been let loose for a quick morning scamper by their owner, who meant no harm whatsoever. As we buried the loose legs, sheets of skin, severed udders and the other unmentionable horrors that are the aftermath of what people so inadequately refer to as dog 'worrying', we were angry, very angry indeed. I blamed city folk in general and was simply unable to see the attack in anything approaching a rational fashion for several days. Then I realised that we had done nothing practical to avoid the problem. So we talked to our neighbours, put up notices and banned all dogs from the archaeological park. Since then we have had no real trouble with dogs.

I think this story illustrates some of the problems inherent in the term 'access', when used in the context of farming and land management. What we really mean by 'access' is surely 'control'. That is the crux of the matter. Now one cannot farm land without also being able to control what takes place on it. In the Wild West the cattle ranchers objected violently to the arrival of homesteaders — who were, in effect New World colonial peasant farmers. In agro-economic terms the ranch vs homestead contest was about intensification versus extensification and the need to produce more food to feed a rapidly growing urban population in the less wild East. In other parts of the world, for example in west Africa, the two types of farmer co-exist: the one providing what the other lacks. They have regular seasonal contacts and the land they farm does not overlap; friction is thereby avoided.

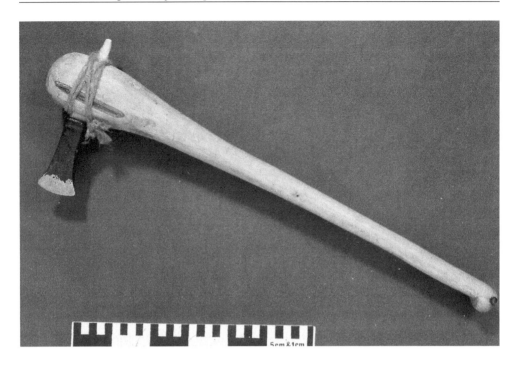

13   Some archaeological experiments gave surprising results. The shape of this rather unusual two-piece wooden haft was based on an example found at Flag Fen in 1989.

Clearing the land

It stands to reason that it's difficult to farm in a forest because the trees get in the way, and they exclude light. In England we have been very good at clearing forest. In fact we have been so good at it that we have removed all traces of the primeval forests that once cloaked the country from Northumberland to Land's End. Our ancient woodlands are managed woodlands which were grown essentially as crops in Saxon and Medieval times, to be sources of firewood, timber and coppice products, such as withies and wattle. True primeval forest now only survives in remoter parts of, for example, highland Scotland. But how were the great hardwood forests of lowland Britain, with their huge oaks and beech trees felled?

It is quite possible to fell a massive forest tree with a light bronze or stone axe, but it takes a long time. My friend and colleague Richard Darrah, who is a skilled woodworker, has just finished making a replica of a Bronze Age boat recently found at Dover. Having used replica Bronze Age tools throughout the experimental reconstruction, Richard reckons it would take a full day for one man to fell a large forest oak. I think there can be little doubt that the light axes of the Neolithic and Bronze Ages were far better adapted to such tasks as hedge-laying, coppicing a stand of hazel and of course carpentry, than to the 'brute force' felling of large forest trees.

14   When used by a trained forester the two-piece handle proved to be very effective. This young tree was felled in about five minutes, but much of this time was spent repairing damage to the lashing around the outside of the haft.

Some axes may not have been used for chopping wood at all — in Brittany many Late Bronze Age axes found in hoards were so tiny and so soft (quantities of lead were used in the alloy) that they must have been votive offerings. At Flag Fen a finely made bronze socketed axe was found lying in what were once muds, with its smashed haft above it (**13**). This method of disposal — the ritualised 'killing' of an artefact — is the treatment that was normally meted out to weapons. Certainly the haft was effective, but impractical when put to use (**14**), and I suggest that this particular axe had been hafted as a weapon rather than a tool.

We know that large forest trees were indeed felled in the Bronze Age — and we have found many at Flag Fen — but I suspect such trees were only chopped down as and when their timber was needed. In other words, they were not chopped down routinely — merely to clear land. Nor were they felled and allowed to season before use (seasoned hardwood is almost too hard to work with a bronze tool). No, timber was felled to be used; it was felled for a specific purpose and, whatever we may think of their appearance, the wooden hafts of felling axes were highly effective (**15**). But there is another, very practical, problem which has important ramifications: forest trees sprout vigorously from their stumps when felled.

Most types of forest management, whether they be geared to the production of timber, poles or wattle, involve the felling of trees and the subsequent care and management of

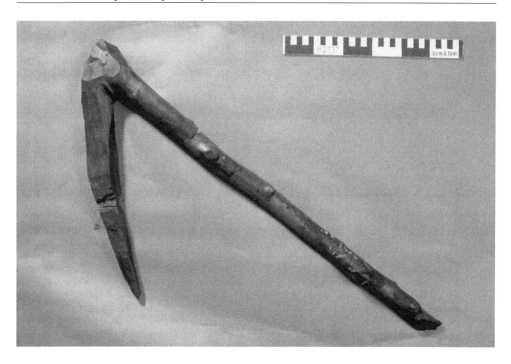

15   This rather ungainly hook-shaped haft is an original Bronze Age piece from Flag Fen. The socketed axe was jammed onto the tapered tip of the hook and the main weight of the haft is around the 'elbow' above. Any lashing would be close to the axehead and would not obstruct the work. This type of one-piece axe haft is commonly found in Bronze Age contexts elsewhere in Europe; it is possible that the two-piece haft was a tomahawk-style battle-axe.

the regrowth that follows. This regrowth is usually extremely vigorous — after all, the tree is fighting to survive after a huge setback — and the poles and wattle that result are fast-grown, straight and clean-grained (which is why they are so useful). Nowadays foresters apply a concentrated chemical poison to the felled tree's stump if they want to prevent re-sprouting. Such things were not available in antiquity, so the only other solution would have been to dig up the stump with as many roots as possible.

Anyone who has had to dig up even a small garden tree and with modern steel spades will know how much work that involves. I shudder to think how long it would take to grub-up a forest tree with ox scapula (shoulder blade) shovels and digging sticks. Burning-out old tree stumps can be very effective, but it is also very time-consuming and labour-intensive. I have found tree stump burning much easier to achieve with an ecologically naughty bucketful of tractor diesel, which of course would not have been available in the Neolithic. No, there has to have been an easier way — and as you will probably have guessed, there was. Or at least I have a theory.

Two summers ago, during the prolonged drought, I was desperate for grass to feed my sheep. I was contemplating the thought of cutting down the fine old hawthorn hedge that bounds one of the fields, when I had the much better idea of letting the animals graze my lawn and some long grass, where I grow spring bulbs. So I fenced the area with electric netting and let the animals in. They thought it was Christmas, and soon the midday silence was broken only by the sound of a hundred jaws contentedly chomping. I went indoors for a quick sandwich.

Fifteen minutes later I returned to find that a lime-tree sapling that I had failed to fence off had been completely stripped of its bark from the ground, to about five feet up the trunk. I gazed in horror at the sheep which were struggling with each other to get at the tree in preference to the lush grass all around them. This example of horticultural incompetence illustrates well that many farm animals would far rather browse (*ie* eat the twigs, bark and leaves of trees and shrubs) than graze. And if there's one thing they prefer above all else, it's the first, sweet and sappy sprouts of regrowth in the spring. Eventually, of course, even the largest old tree will give up the unequal struggle and regrowth will cease — it may take five or more years to kill it, but the end is inevitable.

So sheep, goats and cattle can be used to ring-bark trees and to eat-off secondary growth, but pigs are even more devastating. If confined, and not allowed to wander freely through the forest, they will eat roots, grub up saplings, tear down low branches and generally cause silvan mayhem. With pigs and other farm animals at their disposal, prehistoric farmers had no need to fell trees with axes. Once the process of clearance had been started I suspect it might have proved very difficult to stop.

Floodplain archaeology

While some sites may have been destroyed beneath cities, others may await discovery beneath deposits of colluvium and alluvium (**16**). Anyone who has attempted to go for a winter walk across the flat ploughed fields of the great river valley floodplains of southern Britain will have discovered alluvium. It sticks to one's boots like nothing I know. It builds up on the soles until they feel like a diver's weights: one can kick it clear for two steps of Heaven-sent relief, but then it's back — worse than ever. Personally, having lived with it on excavations for over 20 years, I hate the stuff , but archaeologically it is wonderful — and for two reasons.

Alluvium is the geological name for river-borne flood clay. When rivers are in spate they often turn a pale, opaque buff or pale brown colour. Often this colour comes from tiny particles of soil that were picked up when the river flooded over its banks and flowed across ploughed fields. Sometimes it comes from swollen tributary streams as they cut back their sides. In either or both cases the particles of soil are indeed tiny and are carried in suspension in the water. Now it is a physical fact that water is able to carry a greater load of suspended particles when it is flowing swiftly. As the current decreases, so the load is gradually shed, starting with the heaviest material.

When rivers flow through narrow upland channels the water tumbles and froths and a very heavy load can be carried. But as soon as the stream flows into flatter, more open countryside, it has room to spead out. Huge areas of land can be covered by lowland rivers in times of flood. The slowly moving sheet of water soon starts to deposit the brown-coloured soil it holds in suspension. This material accumulates on the ground below the floodwater as very thin layers of alluvium; closer to the river channel the water moves

16   *This view of an abandoned dig (Etton 1982 excavations a year later) illustrates the problems encountered with river-borne floodclay, or alluvium. The grass to the right is growing on the modern surface above a thin dark band of topsoil. Below is the thick yellow/brown alluvium. The water, to the right is filling a Neolithic ditch which was dug around 3800 BC — before the alluvium above it was laid down.*

faster and the resultant alluvium may be coarser-grained and more silty, but out in the body of the floodplain the great alluvial spread or fan consists of very fine-grained, heavy and sticky clay.

There are two reasons why alluvium is good news in archaeology: first it cloaks, buries and protects. As the river continues to flood so the alluvium gradually builds up, perhaps at the rate of half a millimetre or so a year. When about half a metre of alluvium has built-up, the archaeological deposits below the buried ploughsoil can be considered safe from most types of modern agricultural damage, although some very powerful tractors can pull massive plough-like pan-busters which will penetrate below half a metre. Pan-busters are needed to break up a hard 'pan' of compressed subsoil caused by the weight of modern tractors; this pan can impede drainage and prevent rain from reaching down to plant roots. From a farming perspective, both are disastrous.

As well as burying ancient sites, early episodes of alluviation may coat organic objects, such as wood, twigs and basketry with a layer of clay which retains water and thereby helps to improve preservation.

Those are the good aspects of alluvium. On the down-side one cannot have good protection without making it equally difficult to detect what lies below. In other words,

17   *Removing clay alluvium at Welland Bank, 1997. In this instance the digger is having to remove upwards of half a metre of alluvium to reveal the archaeological deposits below. Without alluvium one would normally expect to remove about 15-23cm (6-9in) of topsoil before encountering* in situ *ancient remains.*

the geophysical techniques employed, for example by television's *Time Team,* to prospect for ancient sites would mostly be useless, given half a metre's alluvial cover; with over a metre almost everything would be hidden. One way around the problem is simply to remove the alluvium in bulk, using powerful earthmoving machines. It's not particularly cheap, but it can be extraordinarily effective (**17**).

I mentioned alluvium and *colluvium*. Colluvium is otherwise known as hill-wash. As with alluvium, the steepness of the slope determines the size of the particles invoved. Thus thick deposits of heavy angular scree accumulate at the foot of steep mountains or cliffs, whereas in rolling chalk downland the particles are very much smaller and the accumulations are thinner. By and large colluvium is an excellent 'coater' or 'buryer' of sites, but it is never found to cover areas as huge as the great alluvial fans of the larger lowland river floodplains.

The large sheets of alluvium, which cover many lowland floodplains, started to form later in the Iron Age. This is a phenomenon that has been observed on archaeological sites in the valleys of the rivers Thames, Great Ouse, Nene, Welland and Trent — and of course in their tributaries. Most people are agreed that this alluviation does not represent something so simple as a sudden increase in annual rainfall. The best explanation can be laid at the door of a now familiar villain: more intensive farming, albeit over two thousand years ago. That was when land was being cleared of trees at an ever-increasing rate, and it was the felled trees' root systems that once bound the soil in place and helped to mop-up rain. Cut down the one and you release the other. An identical process is happening today upstream of Bangladesh, causing the rivers of the Ganges system regularly to burst their banks.

Bare or lightly planted earth is very much more prone to water erosion than woodland or permanent pasture. So the quite dramatic increase in alluviation in the two centuries or so before Christ would suggest that arable farming was rapidly becoming very much more widespread in lowland England at about this time. This is a theme to which I shall return later.

Hunter-gatherers and farmers — the same people?

There is now increasing evidence to suggest that the ways of life of the earliest Neolithic farmers in southern Britain and that of their hunter-gatherer-fisher contemporaries were not grossly dissimilar. Certainly both depended to a very great extent on the exploitation of animals. It is also probable, as we have seen, that the two groups of people may have been related. Whether or not they spoke the same language is, I think, open to discussion, but I find it hard to believe that they could not have made themselves mutually understood.

Archaeologists in Denmark have demonstrated that the earliest Neolithic pattern of farming was highly adapted to a closely forested environment and bore very little resemblance to the open country style of farming that had been so characteristic of the main European 'wave of advance'. However Denmark is by no means the only example of close adaptation to a very distinctive environment. Earlier Neolithic coastal communities in and around the sand hills and low-lying island of the Rhine/Meuse estuary of Holland made extensive use of fishing, fowling, hunting, and also kept livestock. They may have grown cereals locally, but it has also been suggested that these could have been brought into the lowest-lying land from higher ground outside.

If the earlier Neolithic communities of Denmark and Holland, both countries on the edge of the North Sea basin, were capable of adapting their way of life to the peculiarities of local conditions, I can see no reason why their British contemporaries and counterparts did not do so as well. In the Danish case, the pre-Neolithic inhabitants primarily fed themselves on fish and shellfish — as one might expect, given the proximity of the sea. Once the Neolithic way of life had taken a grip, the principal sources of food were land-based — the products of slash-and-burn agriculture, hunting and animal husbandry. But the important point to note is that this new way of life was excellently adapted to a highly forested environment and it would seem reasonable to suppose a close degree of communication between the 'original' hunter-fishers and the 'new' Neolithic farmers / horticulturalists. By no stretch of the imagination could the new Neolithic way of life in Denmark be described as an imposition from outside or, indeed, as a 'revolution'. It was new, yes, but it was well adapted to the local environment and by people, I would suggest, who knew what they were about.

At this point I should perhaps make it clear that water, which causes wood and other organic material to rot in daily life, actually aids its preservation in the un-daily world of archaeology. This is because what one might term 'archaeological water' is not the sort which causes damage: the water of daily life falls as rain and then drips off walls, roofs and lies on the surface of the soil, where it causes wet-rot in gates and fences. The water of daily life is usually well aerated and encourages the growth of fungi and the other agents of rapid destruction. 'Archaeological water' on the other hand does precisely the opposite: it usually derives from the groundwater table, or from stagnant sources such as bogs or fens and is very poorly aerated. Water of this type has the effect of slowing down fungal and bacterial action, almost to stopping point. That is why organic material, such as wood, fabric, seeds and pollen, often survives very well on anaerobic waterlogged sites.

The first farmers in the Fens

What was the way of life of the pre-Neolithic communities in the area we are concerned with here? By rights the Fenland basin and the flat valleys of the rivers draining into it ought to have yielded a wealth of waterlogged and organic-rich Mesolithic sites and finds. To judge from evidence elsewhere in Europe, in its pre-drainage days it was very much the sort of diverse, watery landscape that these small bands of hunter-fishers were so well suited to. Unfortunately, however, most of the Mesolithic sites in Fenland only came to light when the silts and peats soils above them had dried-out and had then been removed by a combination of ploughing and natural erosion. In these circumstances all that we are left with is a scattering of inorganic objects — mainly flint implements — lying on the surface. And it's notoriously hard work to puzzle out why such surface scatters came into existence in the first place.

In the 1970s and '80s English Heritage commissioned a major survey of the Fens, and in their discussion of the results David Hall and John Coles came to a very important conclusion. They noted that Mesolithic hunter-gatherer and Neolithic farming settlements very often occurred on one and the same spot. They also noted that studies of the environmental record, mainly as revealed in pollen grains trapped within growing layers of peat, showed that Mesolithic hunters used fire quite extensively — presumably to make clearings within the forest. In other words, although fishing was plainly very important, it was by no means their sole source of animal protein; deer, elk, wild horse, wild cattle, wild boar and any number of smaller mammals would also have formed an important part of their diet.

The earliest Neolithic farmers must also have hunted and fished, and the emerging evidence now suggests that farmed crops and livestock were introduced very gradually indeed: at first farmed products just supplemented the hunted and gathered food, but after a few generations the farmed food came to dominate. So who were they, these Neolithic farming folk? David Hall and John Coles suggest that the Mesolithic hunter-gatherers and the Neolithic farmers may well have been one and the same people. And for what it is worth, I agree.

So our understanding of the earliest farmers in lowland Britain has come a long way from the notion of Continental 'invaders' bringing with them a foreign pattern of life, which was based principally upon cereal agriculture, which had direct ancestral roots in the Near East and south-eastern Europe. Instead we are beginning to see that the

18   This Bronze Age barrow, exposed in a dykeside at Borough Fen, a few miles north-east of Peterborough, has been buried beneath thick layers of peat and alluvium. The overburden has preserved much of its spectacular orange gravel mound intact — it is clearly visible behind the group of people. The barrow formed part of a group (the bungalow in the background was built on one!) that may have marked the boundary between two quite major, perhaps tribal,territories.

introduction of farming in Britain was a more gradual, and altogether less radical process, in which local, indiginous people played a crucially important role.

If David Hall and John Coles are indeed correct when they suggest that we are talking about ethnically the same group of people hunting and farming, then I think it is also reasonable to suppose that they would have adopted the parts of the farming 'package' of ideas that suited them, and their landscape, the best. And by the same token they would have rejected the things that didn't work. Given a tradition of clearing forest — albeit on a small scale — and of managing animals, I would suggest that they initially opted for livestock or pastoral farming.

The concept of cereal agriculture or horticulture may well have arrived quite early, but I do not think it became of much economic significance for a very long time indeed. As I read it, the evidence suggests that cereal growing on any scale did not become significant until well into the Iron Age — when we find those huge sheets of alluvium being laid-down. And that was some three and a half millennia after the early Neolithic.

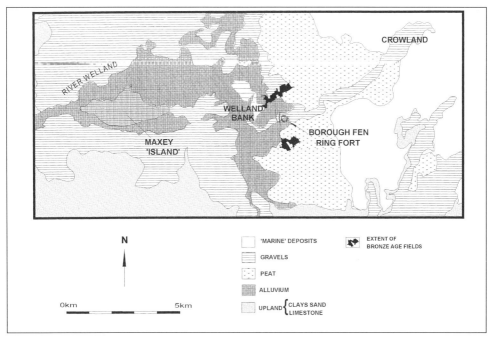

19   *Map of the lower Welland valley and Fenland margins showing the Crowland 'peninsula' and the Maxey 'island'.*

Into the middle Neolithic

The old view of the Neolithic 'revolution' was quite correct when it stated that the switch to a Neolithic way of life allowed or facilitated the construction of large communal monuments. It used to be thought that these monuments were built because people had more leisure in which to indulge in such things. Perhaps today we would take a rather different view: farming folk probably had rather *less* leisure than their hunter-fisher equivalents, but there were many more of them and they were able to focus their energies within an altogether smaller home territory. The end result was an extraordinary harvest of round barrows, long barrows, causewayed enclosures (about which more shortly) and other, less readily defined, field monuments.

I think most archaeologists would now agree that the emergence of field monuments from the fourth millennium BC onwards has to do with territories of one sort or another. Round barrows may have marked the edges of tribal or family lands (**18**), long barrows may have been placed at their centres and causewayed enclosures may have been sited on the edge of habitable land. Or there may be different explanations for each type of field monument in various parts of the country. All are territorial markers of one sort or another. Our next task is to consider what was being marked-out and why it was significant to the world of the farmer.

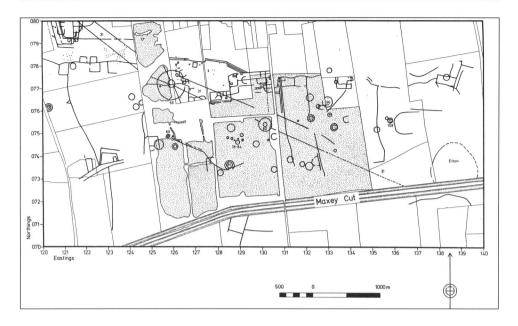

20   *A map of cropmarks near the 'island' village of Maxey in the Welland valley. The long straight ditches belong to Neolithic 'cursus' monuments and the large double ring-ditch (59) is the great central Maxey henge, also of Neolithic date.*

A very special place: Etton

I must now move from the general to the particular, away from the Dark Age that is the earliest Neolithic into a time, the middle Neolithic, for which evidence — and very high-quality evidence — is accumulating with increasing rapidity. I want to discuss a so-called causewayed enclosure at Etton, some 3 miles (5km) north of Peterborough in the floodplain of the river Welland (**19**), just south of the borders of the modern counties of Cambridgeshire and Lincolnshire. It's an extraordinarily rich archaeological landscape, comprising hundreds of important field monuments, of which Etton is, I think, the most important (**20**).

We excavated at Etton for six years, between 1982 and 1987 and were able to reveal about 80% of the site. Today all that remains is the 20% we could not excavate, which lies beneath the bank of a modern canalised river; the rest has been removed — destroyed, I will not mince my words — by gravel extraction.

The site was first revealed in 1976 when it was spotted from the air as a mark in growing crops. The year was one of the driest on record and the roots of the crop had to penetrate deep below the thick layers of alluvium beneath the topsoil. The crop growing directly above the Neolithic ditch was slightly more lush than the rest of the field and this showed-up as a very faint mark on the air photos (**21**). In addition to the Neolithic ditch there were other, much darker, marks which appeared to swirl around the ditch, to the north. When seen from the air, the ditch appeared to resemble a string of enormous sausages laid on the

21   Buried beneath thick layers of clay alluvium, the Etton causewayed enclosure showed-up very faintly on this aerial photograph. A relict stream channel belt is marked by a series of dark swirls and the Neolithic segmented ditch is visible below it, to the left (photo by S J Upex, Nene Valley Research Committee).

ground to form a squashed circle of about 200m in diameter. The swirl of marks north of the circular enclosure was a series of stream channels belonging to one of the ancient courses of the river Welland.

Its appearance as a 'string of sausages' was caused by the fact that the ditch was not dug in a continuous length; in effect it was a series of oval or oblong pits which were separated from each other by short, undug 'causeways'. There have been all sorts of explanations for this strange way of digging a ditch. One widely held explanation took a very simple view: that the segments represented the work of different gangs. The trouble with this hypothesis was that it failed to explain why the separate segments of ditch were not then joined together to form a single encircling ditch. It assumes a level of technical incompetence that flies in the face of what we know about Neolithic builders and engineers. No, the reason the enclosure ditch of causewayed enclosure was dug in segments was quite simply that that was the way people *wanted* them to be dug — and there is absolutely no evidence that they were abandoned, unfinished.

Causewayed enclosures are very distinctive on air photos. Etton is quite small and only has a single interrupted ditch around its perimeter. Others may be three or four times as large and can have two or three or even four sets of encircling ditches. In Britain causewayed enclosures are mainly confined to Wessex and the south-east, but they also occur widely on the continent, in Scandinavia, France and Germany.

One striking aspect of causewayed enclosures is that they were often positioned slightly off-centre, but within or upon prominent features of the landscape. The most famous of them all, the great monument at Windmill Hill, near Avebury in Wiltshire, does not 'crown' the hill, like an Iron Age hillfort. Instead it sits slightly to one side, rather like a jauntily worn beret.

At Etton the enclosure is positioned to one side of an old meander; it was not placed on the slightly drier ground near the meander's centre. There are numerous other examples of such eccentric positioning. But why was this? One explanation, and the one I prefer, is that the 'prominent features of the landscape' as I rather stuffily called them — the hills, promontories, rivers and so forth — were already sacred or significant in some way. Maybe, like Ayres Rock in Australia, they were viewed by the local aboriginal population as very special places that linked the living with the dead and this world with the next. They could also provide a symbol of communal identity — like, on a far larger scale, the White Cliffs of Dover to the English, or Mount Fuji to the Japanese. If that were the case then it might well be seen as inappropriate actually to dominate the special or sacred landscape feature with a new, man-made monument. Humility can be a sound idea in such situations.

The role of causewayed enclosures

What were causewayed enclosures, and why were they built? The first point to note is that they do not appear to have served a practical or utilitarian purpose. Where they occur, they are often the earliest monument (in the sense of earthwork) in the area, but they are rarely located in a position that one could describe as 'user-friendly'. In other words they may, like Etton, be positioned on very low-lying land, liable to floods, or else, like Windmill Hill, they were placed atop a steep hill. Neither location is easy of access and it seems most unlikely that they could have been used, for example, to hold regular livestock markets or as a secure store for grain over winter. So far as we know none of the British causewayed enclosures was used as a straightforward settlement, with houses, byres, storage pits and the usual paraphernalia of village life.

Now it seems to be a fact of archaeological life that, when there is no obvious explanation for some phenomenon, then archaeologists fall back on 'ritual' — which in this instance we might translate near enough as 'religion'. And why not? If religion is not about the inexplicable it is about nothing. So who were these early farmers worshipping and what do their beliefs tell us about them, as people? To approach these questions we must return to the ancient landscape: that was the complex and very variable setting which formed the backdrop to both daily life and to the world of ritual and religion.

The modern landscape around Etton is very low-key and very English. Indeed it is very low-key in that it is flat: there are a few hedges and even fewer trees, and the limestone hills of Leicestershire and Rutland are just visible as a thin bluish frieze on the western horizon. It is also very English in that it has been devastated in recent years: hedges have been removed wholesale, trunk roads have been forced through it and most of the trees have died-back to form great 'stags heads' — a result of land drainage and de-watering brought about by the extraction of gravel, quarried to build the ever-expanding City of Peterborough. But if creeping urbanism provides the final threat to this gentle landscape, there have been many before.

One hundred and fifty years ago the poet John Clare lived in Helpston whose stubby church steeple can clearly be seen from Etton. His gravestone in Helpston churchyard bears the epitaph: *A Poet Is Born Not Made*. Although strictly speaking the lower Welland valley around Etton and Helpston cannot be considered true Fenland it was in its natural, undrained, state a very wet, flat river valley with numerous small woods, ponds and meandering streams. And the point where the river valley ceases and the fen starts is far from certain. Some people refer to this low, flat plain around the fringes of the Fens as 'skirtland'.

Clare loved this countryside: he would linger in its secluded damp places and was appalled by the changes brought about by the Enclosure Acts. To read his description of hills, trees and bushes being levelled and moles hung as traitors one could easily he was describing the landscape devastation of the late 1960s and '70s. He describes the brook, which was still running, as being naked and chill. The last time I saw the brook it had been dry for at least two years.

I mention this catalogue of ecological horrors merely to emphasis how very difficult it is for us to imagine what it would have been like to have lived in Clare country six thousand years ago. First of all we must remove all thoughts of the modern river Welland and its canalised tributaries and flood-relief channels, and replace it with a braided — multi-coursed — series of streams which snaked their way down the valley. In summertime many of the streams would be dry, but in winter huge areas of the valley would be inundated and only the highest parts would remain dry. We will call these high spots 'islands', as they were probably only true islands in the wettest months of a wet winter.

4 Maccus' Island

Excavating Etton

The most important of the low-lying and very flat 'islands' in the Welland valley is today known as Maxey (from the Saxon: *Macuseige* meaning, 'dry land or an island belonging to a man names Maccus'). Today the picturesque limestone-built village of Maxey sits at the centre of the 'island' which falls away very gradually on all sides. The 'island' was composed of freely draining limestone gravel and the soils would have been light and of good quality. In a situation like Maxey, human habitation tended to concentrate on the highest and driest parts of the 'island', in a manner somewhat reminiscent of the 'tells' of south-eastern Europe.

Maxey church sits on top of a large mound which I suspect — but cannot prove — may even have been a Neolithic barrow. Near the church run two parallel ditches of a so-called 'cursus' monument and two fields away is an extraordinary complex of 'henge' monuments. Both the cursus and the henge monuments date to the centuries on either side of 2000 BC, in the later Neolithic period. Unlike Stonehenge, the Maxey henge was built of timber.

Air photos of the southern fringes of the 'island' around the cursus and henge monuments reveal a bewildering profusion of smaller henge-like monuments and literally dozens of Bronze Age round barrows. Prehistoric landscapes of this sort are known elsewhere in Britain and have been dubbed 'ritual landscapes'. For want of anything better I will also use the term.

The earliest component of the Maxey ritual landscape, the Etton causewayed enclosure, was not actually located on the 'island' itself. Instead, it sat about fifty metres 'off-shore' on its own mini-'island', surrounded on all sides by rivers, or old stream courses. This location, just off the edge of the main 'island' says much, I believe, about the site's original purpose.

The air photos of Etton that were taken in 1976 gave no clue to any detail — all that showed through the thick deposit of blanketing alluvium was the faint 'string of sausages' effect of the interrupted ditch around the outside of the enclosure. But when we started excavation we soon realised how well the alluvium had preserved the archaeological deposits beneath it. Then to our huge excitement we discovered that the deepest layers within the ditch were still waterlogged and contained thousands of pieces of wood and other organic finds. Some of the woodchips from the ditch provided reliable radiocarbon dates that show the site was first built and used around 3800 BC. By any reckoning that is

22   Organised chaos: a working view of the team excavating the waterlogged ditch deposits at Etton, 1982. Note the dark peaty soil in which the Neolithic wood is preserved.

a very early date and it shows that the site was constructed just a few centuries after the initial appearance of farming.

The presence of waterlogged material caused us all sorts of headaches. The nearby quarry was now in operation and water had been removed on a massive scale to allow gravel extraction to take place. So somehow we had to excavate rapidly drying wood and keep it wet at the same time. We used vast amounts of newspaper, plastic sheeting, foam sponges — anything that gave us mobile sources of instant wetness. The scene in the wet areas during excavation resembled a madman's kitchen (**22**), with archaeologists rushing from one spot to another with buckets, watering cans, sponges and clipboards. This seeming chaos was actually extremely well organised by Maisie and it has all proved worth the effort: never before has so large an assemblage of Neolithic woodworking debris been excavated under controlled conditions (**23, 24**). It took four years to complete, and in retrospect it must be seen for what it was: a major feat of archaeological salvage.

In a strange way, almost the most important result of our work at Etton was a negative one. Normally speaking to claim that one's excavations have revealed 'negative evidence' is another way of saying that they have failed. It's a phrase I try to avoid at all costs. Archaeologists who never find anything are rather like racing drivers who drive with caution: they are worthy but unemployed.

Now we have already seen that on most rural sites in Britain the archaeological features lie directly below the ploughsoil, and modern powerful farm implements can easily penetrate right through the topsoil into the archaeological levels. As a result most rural

23   *Etton 1985. By this time the pumping out of the quarry next to the excavation had caused the ancient wood in the ditch to become seriously degraded. Even sunlight would cause damage to now very fragile wood. The dark area in the foreground has had its shelter removed to allow a rapid photograph to be taken.*

24   *Etton: work beneath the shelter. Here an archaeologist draws a plan of the wood exposed on the ditch bottom. Note the long, straight rods that probably resulted from the regular harvesting and cutting-back of coppice alder and willow.*

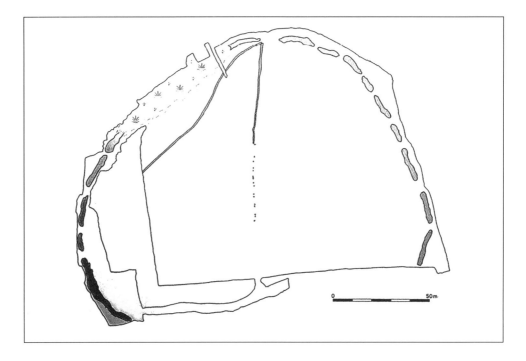

25   A simplified plan of the causewayed enclosure at Etton, showing the segmented enclosure ditch and the central fence or partition.

sites in southern Britain have suffered severe plough damage in recent years. The trouble is, however, that it is nearly impossible to quantify this damage: have post-holes, for example, been truncated or 'shortened', or have they been completely removed? Often it is very hard to say. But at Etton, because the site had been covered in alluvium from later prehistoric times, we could be certain: there had been no plough-damage whatsoever.

When we removed the alluvium and the thin layer of ancient topsoil sealed beneath it, we found no evidence for houses: there were no wall posts, porch or doorway posts, nor even hearths. We could be quite categoric: Etton had never been a prehistoric village or settlement; people undoubtedly stayed there from time to time, but they never *lived* there — and that was very important.

A very organised space

The layout of the enclosure was simple and consistent (**25**). The outer, segmented ditch formed a slightly squashed circle, a small part of which lay buried and invisible beneath the bank of the Maxey Cut flood-relief channel, which clipped the enclosure along its southern edge. We know nothing about this southern side of the enclosure but, as we have seen, it probably only represents about 20% of the whole. Maybe in a hundred years time the Maxey Cut will be replaced by a new channel, in which case archaeologists of the future will be able to examine the last surviving fragment of the monument.

26   *This view gives an impression of the size of the Etton enclosure. It is taken from the centre of the main northern entranceway. In the foreground, to the left, is the central partitioning ditch and, in the distance, is the bank of the Maxey Cut.*

At the apex of the northern course of the enclosure ditch was a wide gap or entranceway. Immediately upon entering the enclosure (**26**) the visitor would have faced a tunnel-like gateway constructed from large oak posts that had been trimmed square and then set vertically in the ground, edge-to-edge to form two massive, parallel walls about a foot thick. Presumably there was a floor or balcony above the gateway, or there would be no need to employ such big posts.

On leaving the enclosure by way of the main northern entrance, the visitor would have been confronted by a wide, but probably shallow and boggy, stream channel. So access to the enclosure would always have been difficult. I suspect that children who had yet to undergo their initiation rites into adulthood would not have been let in.

Directly inside the northern gateway was a fence which ran north-south and divided the interior of the enclosure into two halves. The eastern half had its own entranceway, facing due east, into the rising sun. The western half also had its own entrance; again it faced the cardinal point of the compass, and it was served or protected by a small gatehouse — the only *bona fide* building within the enclosure.

Deliberate deposition

After several seasons spent excavating Etton I began to gain the impression that nothing we revealed had been left to chance; that everything we found had been put there. It was

27   *Some of the small filled pits at Etton were marked by the placing of valuable objects high in the filling this one was capped by a magnificent quartzite axe polishing stone, which may have been brought to Etton from Derbyshire.*

a strange feeling, almost as if the people who had used the site were getting us to write their prehistory the way they wanted it expressed. It was as if the past was directing the work of the modern archaeologists. Altogether it was a very peculiar — rational folk would say absurd — feeling, and I've never been able to rid myself of it completely.

The eastern half of the enclosure contained a large number of small pits. Each pit was in effect a small, vertical-sided hole, just large enough to hold a modern bucket. The evidence suggests that each hole had been dug and filled as part of the same operation. The filling consisted of soil mixed with pottery, flint tools and animal bone, which had quite often been burnt. It was not unusual to find that a large object, such as an axe or in one case an axe polishing stone (**27**), had been placed at the very top of the filling. I am convinced, for a variety of reasons, that these holes were not rubbish pits; they were all dug and filled with some care and sometimes contained valuable objects; most important of all, they never inter-cut one another (**28**). In other words, their presence must have been marked or mapped in some way.

The enclosure ditch on the eastern side (**29**) showed clear evidence for digging and back-filling in at least three separate and clearly defined episodes. Special 'offerings' of carefully placed items were positioned along the centre of the base of the ditch (**30**). These 'offerings' included, for example, a human skull, an inverted, severed fox skull, complete pots (both upside-down and right-side-up) and many other peculiar items that could not conceivably have found their way into the ditch by accident. The 'offerings' were then

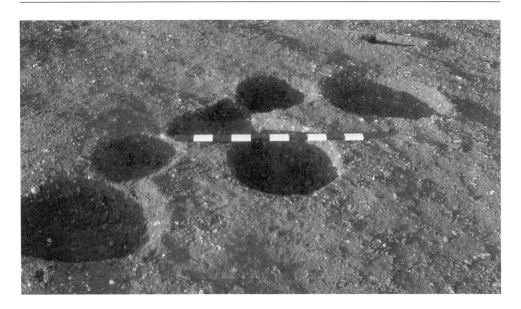

28   *A close group of six small pits at Etton (the scale is 1m long). It is tempting to suggest that each pit in the group represents an individual person. None of the pits inter-cut which would suggest that they were dug and filled at about the same time. Perhaps the people represented by the pits were connected in some way, most probably by family ties.*

29   *A view along the eastern side of the Etton enclosure ditch from the main northern entranceway. One of the undug 'causeways' between different segments of ditch is visible behind the nearest figure.*

30   *An example of a group of 'offerings' that were placed on the base of the enclosure ditch at Etton. In the foreground is an inverted fox skull, behind it is an inverted round-bottomed pottery vessel which resembles a human skull, beyond that is a decorated antler comb and beyond that near the top of a picture is a small round jar, place right-way-up in the ground (it is visible as a very small ring).*

buried and the ditch filled in. At some point in the future — perhaps a generation or two later — the people would return to the ditch, remove the backfilling over the first offering, very carefully so as not to disturb it, and place a second offering in the ground. Then that too would be buried. The process was then repeated for a third and even a fourth time.

The so-called butt-ends, *ie* the ends of the ditch segments on either side of an intervening causeway, were nearly always the scene of extra-special or memorable 'offerings', such as human skulls or skull fragments or even round stones made to represent human heads. I would suggest that these butt-end offerings were considered very important as they marked the special significance of the new length of ditch. They were a flag or a label identifying both the new segment, and the group of people who controlled the rites that took place within and around it.

It is possible that each segment of ditch may have represented different 'guilds' of craftsmen or something of the sort, but I find that unlikely. Surely the symbolism surrounding craft guilds would be quite easy to identify in the ground: potters would 'offer' pots, flint-knappers, flint and so forth. Instead, each segment of ditch was filled with the same broad repertoire of 'offerings', which were generally to do with death or the Afterlife. After much thought I came to the conclusion that the ditch segments represented individual families — or kin-groups to use the anthropological term.

Human beings have always been competitive and the various families would have competed amongst themselves to place the most unusual or valuable items in the ground in order to increase their social standing or prestige. The small filled pits seemed to cluster around the ditch segments and we may again suppose that these represented individuals, within each family group. The actual bodies were presumably buried within long barrows nearer to the farm or village where the deceased had lived. The eastern half of the enclosure was where the dead person's soul made its journey to the Next World, to join the ancestors. We might suppose that this journey was seen as a new beginning, a fresh start, something to view optimistically — hence the focus on the sun's *rising*.

A recurrent theme: querns

One of the small pits in the eastern half had a most unusual filling. There was very little room for soil, since the pit was almost entirely filled by a single massive saddle quern. Querns are stones for grinding corn into flour, and in the Neolithic and Bronze Age, before the invention of the more efficient rotary or mill-wheel-like quern, the person preparing the meal knelt astride the main or bottom stone and rubbed the grain against it, using a smaller top stone which was gripped firmly in both hands. As time passed, the bottom stone developed a characteristically U-shaped profile, reminiscent of a saddle.

The top of the pit held the top stone which had been deliberately placed in the ground on its side — in which position, of course, it would have been useless (**31**). We removed it from the ground only to find that it had been placed directly above its original top stone which had been paced at the bottom of the pit (**32**). So the bottom stone was on its side above the top stone. Surely this is saying something? The world turned upside-down? To me, it is saying that these quernstones have done their rubbing and have deliberately been taken out of domestic circulation, for use in the Next World. Yes, on reflection, the world

*31   This saddle quern (corn grinding stone) was placed on its edge in a small pit at Etton. Placed
in this position, it could not possibly have been used and its upper part would have been
visible above ground.*

*32   Below the saddle quern in the small pit at Etton was the topstone that acompanied it. The
normal position of the two stones in domestic life had been reversed. This was a symbolic act
intended to remove them from circulation within the everyday world.*

turned upside-down.

It was more usual to find that saddle querns had been smashed and were placed in segments of the enclosure ditch with some care. Perhaps they served to mark out different parts of individul ditch segments — as if delimiting sub-groups within broader kin-groups (or, to put it differently, nuclear families within an extended family). The point I am trying to make is that the quernstone has come to represent the family unit — it does not necessarily mean that each family consumed large quantities of flour. In fact I would not be at all surprised to learn that flour was only consumed at special feasts.

Querns are very characteristic of earlier Neolithic sites, but nobody has yet published a systematic study of the way they were treated before burial in the ground. Sometimes, but by no means always, the stones were worn out and were discarded, but not without some care. In many instances, and here Etton is not alone, the stones had been deliberately smashed. At Hurst Fen, near Mildenhall in Suffolk, the querns had been treated in this way and it has always been assumed that they were part of the domestic rubbish. But when one thinks about the site's location, a small sand 'island' surrounded by very wet peat fen, one wonders whether it would have been possible to have grown cereals there at all. Certainly the stones must have been brought there from some distance away. Does it really make sense for a community to carry items as heavy as grain and querns out to a Fenland 'island', and then smash the stones and bury them in small pits? I think not. I do not believe that the smashed querns at Hurst Fen or indeed at Etton were used to grind grain for ordinary meals. Both sites were in spots that were far too wet and low-lying. By this stage in the Neolithic querns had become more important as symbols, than as useful objects of daily life.

The symbolism behind everyday things

If the way querns were treated was peculiar, something similar and equally odd happened to axes, too. At Etton finely polished greenstone axes from the Lake District quarries at Langdale had been deliberately smashed in a way that could not be the result of an accident while wood-working. These axes were beautiful objects in their own right and while it is possible to speculate on their symbolic meaning — man's control of the forest etc. — it would seem more probable that they had evolved to become symbols of an individual person's identity and prestige. They are found quite frequently within the small filled-in pits which seem to have been associated with the lives and achievements of individual people. So the axe can be seen to relate to the individual, while the quern represents the family. We are beginning to crack the code.

If we can ascribe a symbolic role to items as mundane as axes and querns, is it possible that other artefacts of daily life had a dual purpose? Of course the answer is yes. I would go further: I do not believe that any object was placed in a hole in the ground in pre-Roman times simply as a means of disposal. Indeed, I would go further still: I remain to be convinced that prehistoric people even possessed the concept of rubbish.

Everything was expressive of something else. Meat cut off the animal bones that were carefully placed in the ditch had fed the farmer's family, and the bone was duly returned to the ground to continue or restart the cycle of birth, growth and sustenance. It was not 'disposed of' in the garbage, with hygienic efficiency. In other words, the bones that we found buried in the ground were symbols of far more than just food.

The western side of the enclosure was altogether different. Here there were far fewer small filled pits and the enclosure ditch showed less evidence for repeated recutting and in-filling. Its segments too were less regular in shape and size. Above all else, the lowest levels of the ditch were waterlogged and produced over 6,000 pieces of worked wood, including chopped sticks, numerous woodchips and so on. The 'offerings' or placed deposits were altogether different. Attention was still focused on butt-ends which produced some remarkable finds, such as an inverted bowl placed on a birch bark mat, but the careful arrangement of items down the ditch centre was never found. By contrast, the ditch deposits on the west side looked more like the actual debris of woodworking; much of which derived not from working great timbers, such as the oak posts of the north entranceway, but from 'bodging', or working coppice — in other words, fashioning wattle hurdles, fences etc.

Within and amongst the woodchips we found small heaps of animal bone, which usually derived from a single animal — often a sheep — but which missed certain key pieces, such as a skull or leg bone. These bones were very fresh and showed clear signs of having had the meat cut off them. It is hard to resist the thought that they represent the remains of feasts that were ritually returned to Mother Earth — or something of the sort

1   *The Main Drove, Fengate 1974, looking east, with the Fens in the background. The two ditches at the centre marked the course of a Bronze Age livestock droveway which ran at right-angles to the edge of the Fens. The green field is now the site of the Peterborough Power Station and the wetland edge lies behind the large bush in the middle background.*

2   *A closer view of the Main Drove, Fengate 1974, looking east. The dark pit in the foreground is modern. Note the regular layout of the system, with clear right-angled corners and neatly parallel ditches. This might indicate that the drove and enclosures associated with it were laid-out as a single operation.*

3   *The main Drove, Fengate 1976, looking east, towards the Fens. After another two seasons work, the sheer size and scale of the Bronze Age droveway system was beginning to be apparent.*

4   *The main Drove, Fengate 1976, looking west. The range pole is lying in the Main Drove; another lies in an entranceway into a subsidiary or 'feeder' drove, lower left. In the background the factories of Peterborough New Town are beginning to encroach on the excavations.*

5   *Fengate, 1973 excavations: the early Bronze Age 'race'. The black and white (2m) scale has been placed at the southern end of the race between the two side ditches.*

6   *Fengate, 1973 excavations: looking south along the 'race'; the excavators are working on Neolithic features that pre-dated it.*

7   *Fengate, 1973 excavations: the southern or business end of the 'race'. This was where livestock were sorted in three directions.*

8   *(Opposite) Fengate, 1973 excavations: a three-way corner entranceway at the north end of the Early Bronze Age field with the 'race' just visible at the end of the main N-S ditch at the very top of the picture.*

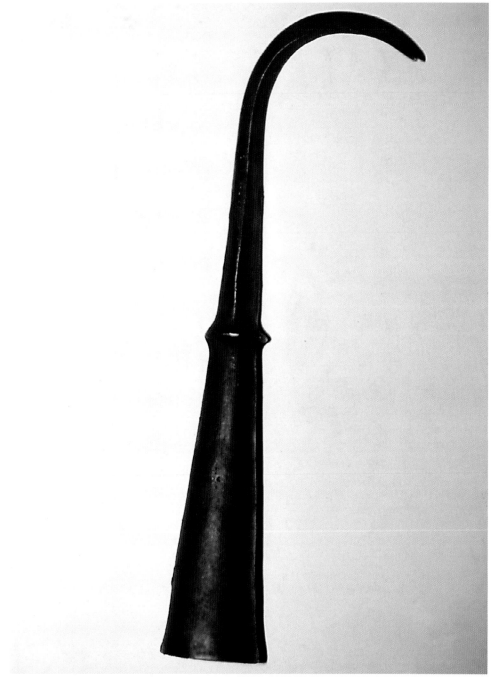

9　*Middle Bronze Age bronze 'flesh-hook' from Flag Fen. These objects have been found in close association with cauldrons and it is thought that they may have been used to fish pieces of meat from out of stews at feasts. The Flag Fen flesh-hook is a beautifully fashioned piece which emphasises the high status of meat-eating in the Bronze Age. Length: 145mm (5¾ inches).*

10   One third of a Bronze Age (c1300 BC) alder wheel from Flag Fen, Peterborough, when first
      exposed in the excavation. The wheel is visable as a crescent in the patch of water (lower left).

11   *These slight parallel stains at Welland Bank Quarry are possibly the oldest marks left by a wheeled vehicle in Britain. They date to the Late Bronze Age and can be followed for over 100m (*photo courtesy APS*).*

12   Close-up of a Late Bronze Age wheel-rut after excavation. At this point the vehicle had stuck in mud and the forking effect of the ruts was probably produced by rocking to and fro to escape (photo courtesy APS).

13   The great earthwork at Welland Bank Quarry when first revealed. This view is taken from the wetland side of the earlier Bronze Age (c1500 BC) earthwork which is thought to mark the boundary between fen and dry land. Here the digger is removing alluvial flood-clay to reveal a gravel bank accompanied by a peat-filled ditch. The ground in the foreground is pale and clean, whereas that beyond the bank (where the digger is working) consists of 'dark earth', rich in charcoal and settlement debris.

14   A view of the Welland Bank earthwork taken from the dryland side. The 'dark earth' in the foreground laps up to and over the gravel bank. The earthwork was probably constructed several centuries before the 'dark earth' came to be laid-down sometime around 600-800 BC. In the background a mini-digger is working in the lower deposits of the earthwork's ditch.

15   The Welland Bank Bronze Age earthwork during excavation. The buried soil below the bank is being exposed in the foreground. The ditch (section marked by many white labels) can be seen in the background.

16   *The 'dark earth' at Welland Bank quarry was a mixture of charcoal and domestic rubbish that lay undisturbed, hidden below overlying river-borne alluvial flood clay. It had a distinct edge which is clearly visible in this view and it is possible that the area of 'dark earth' was bounded by a hedge which has left no archaeological trace.*

17   *(Opposite) A drainage dyke cut through the Iron Age ring-fort at Borough Fen (c1350 BC). This photograph shows the archaeological soil scientist, Dr Charles French, examining a thick layer of 'dark earth' that has been exposed directly above the red and white ranging pole. It is possible that the 'dark earth' was deliberately enriched with manure, household refuse and hearth-sweepings to improve its working qualities as an arable soil.*

18   *When we examined it closely we found that the later Bronze Age 'dark earth' at Welland Bank quarry contained literally thousands of potsherds, pieces of burnt stone, fired clay and fragments of animal bone. This material was plotted, recorded and removed from site as part of a detailed 'finger-tip search', or surface survey.*

19a&b Two views of excavation underway in the ditch of the Welland Bank rectangular enclosure. The filling of the large outer ditch contained very little domestic or settlement debris and it would appear that the enclosure had been constructed to contain livestock, probably belonging to the inhabitants of the Late Bronze Age settlement nearby. Maybe the enclosure would have provided protection against cattle rustlers.

20   *The timbers of the Flag Fen post alignment (1300-900 BC). The five rows of posts comprising the alignment formed a barrier and a roadway across the waters of Flag Fen, linking the dryland field systems of Fengate, to the west, and Northey, to the east.*

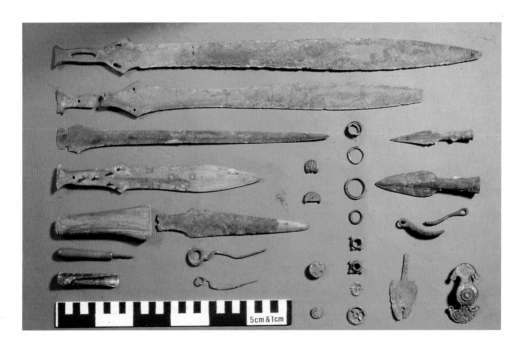

21   *A small selection of Bronze and Early Iron Age objects from Flag Fen.*

— within the confines of the ditch. 'Sheep heaps', as we called them during the dig, were never found within isolated features of the interior, such as pits.

Loose human bones were found in the ditch on both sides of the central partitioning fence, but unlike the animal bones these were worn and abraded and some bore clear signs of having been gnawed by dogs. Normally one might expect it to have been *vice versa*: abraded meat bones and fresh human bones. The explanation is probably that some corpses were subjected to excarnation, or exposure on a platform — a process whereby flesh is removed by carrion crows and the soul is thought to ascend to the Next World with the birds. Once the flesh has been removed, the bones that remain are considered to be of no importance.

Structured space

The western side of the enclosure produced one intriguing piece of evidence that is very directly relevant to our theme. For reasons of chemistry that I do not pretend fully to understand, phosphates produced by decaying bodies or manure somehow 'lock-on' to tiny particles in the soil for a very long time indeed. By great good fortune the soils in the Peterborough region have the right alkalinity to allow enhanced phosphate levels to survive for millennia. Samples were taken from the west area and were analysed for phosphates. The results showed an increased, but even, concentration of phosphate over part of the western enclosure. The pattern of phosphate enhancement suggested that it was the result of the direct manuring of the ground by animals. There was no evidence for areas of extra-high enhancement which might have been the result had muck heaps been present. It would not appear that animals were necessarily kept there for extended periods.

A few hawthorn twigs from the enclosure ditch near the area of phosphate enhancement had grown in a strange L-shaped fashion which is often the effect that hedge-trimming has on growing wood. The presence of a hedge would help to explain the absence of post-built fences and for the sharp decline in soil phosphate levels halfway across the western part of the enclosure. So what does all this suggest? The main conclusion was that part of the western enclosure had been used to hold a few animals, most probably to be used for the feasts that also took place there, to judge from the 'sheep heaps'.

A picture is slowly beginning to emerge. The east side of the enclosure is about families and family ties; it is also about the journey out of, and into, this world. But it does not appear to be about this world or daily life. That is the province of the western side. That is where the feasting took place and the animals were stored. Perhaps that was the place where ceremonies to do with, for example, completing apprenticeships took place. It is interesting too that woodland crafts, such as the working of coppice products, took place actually within the enclosure ditch which, like the woods themselves, ran around the perimeter or boundary of the farmed landscape. So the world within the enclosure might have been seen as a miniature, formalised expression of the greater world outside. Symbolism, it would seem, is everywhere.

Public and Private — together

We have seen that the interior of the enclosure at Etton was divided into two halves. But what else did they represent — what did they mean to people at the time? It seems to me that the western half, where there were indications for some livestock being held and much feasting, was the side of the enclosure given-over to public gatherings. This was where people met to celebrate marriages, exchange animals and generally socialise, although probably in a formal manner, as would befit such a very special place.

The eastern half of the enclosure may have been very different. This was where souls began their journey to the Next World. It was a space given over to those more private, sometimes even solitary activities that today are mainly confined to the cemetery or churchyard. Doubtless the picture was very more complex than I have sketched it here, but I feel reasonably confident that the public versus private partition of the enclosure — a division which after all affects all of our lives — was of fundamental significance. It is a theme to which I shall return when we come to discuss Flag Fen.

It is very difficult to be precise about when the gatherings within causewayed enclosures took place. Sometimes the presence of carbonised hazelnut shells and acorns has been taken to indicate autumn gatherings — but again it could be argued that nuts and acorns are easily stored. At Etton evidence from tree-rings suggests that coppiced wood from the western part of the enclosure ditch was cut in the latter part of the year, *ie* in late summer or autumn. Moreover, there are good reasons to suppose that the site would have been too wet in winter. Reliability of access must surely be an important concept in terms of ritual gatherings arranged some time in advance: if the place were to be flooded when the important people from the different communities gathered together, someone — or rather some group — would be bound to lose face.

Traditionally late summer or early autumn is a good time in the farming year to hold assemblies. Crops would just have been harvested, surplus stock would be ready for slaughter and the heaviest work of the year would have been finished. It is the time of year when even today many livestock markets are at their busiest.

How often was Etton used?

Human societies have marriage laws to avoid in-breeding. Livestock farmers have similar rules for the same reason. If a herd or flock becomes in-bred the effects appear quite rapidly: there is a failure of young animals to thrive, the conception rate drops and genetic disorders — such as cleft palate and birth defects — become more frequent. It was in everyone's interest to avoid in-breeding and that could best be achieved by exchanging animals with communities outside the immediate vicinity. But how often did these meetings take place?

The archaeological evidence from Etton and other causewayed enclosures suggests that their 'use' for gatherings was indeed episodic. But this evidence — almost by definition — comes from below the ground alone. We simply don't know what was happening in those cases where meetings took place that did not involve the wholesale digging-out and back-filling of enclosure ditch segments.

Now in simple terms of practical farming it is ludicrous to expect problems of in-breeding to be avoided if the three or so recutting ceremonies represented the totality of Etton's 'use'— in other words, if the only occasions when Etton was visited by large gatherings of people and animals was when earth was moved and archaeologically visible material was placed in the ground. If that were indeed the case I cannot conceive how new blood lines were to be brought in to the flocks and herds in the area.

Regular exchange of livestock is necessary to avoid in-breeding. It is simply no use if one 'imports' new blood into a herd or flock every five or ten years; even if one is running a modern so-called 'closed' flock, as a means of minimising the impact of diseases such as scrapie, one would have to buy-in a new ram every two or three years. In very round figures, a ram can tup (serve) about 50 ewes and has a prime working life of six or seven seasons; so to maintain a flock of 300 ewes one would need, at the very least, to obtain a new ram every year. In practice, most flocks are slightly over-stocked with rams because it is in nobody's interests to have untupped, barren ewes at lambing time.

Calculations of the sort I have just sketched-in are minimum figures only: in antiquity, for example, it is *highly* improbable that people even attempted to keep 'closed' flocks and I would not be at all surprised if as much as 25% of the ewes in a given flock changed at regular intervals. If this was the order of magnitude of livestock movements, then I would consider that a minimum of one annual gathering would be required in order to satisfy the requirement to exchange animals. As for those other animals — human beings – common-sense suggests that annual social gatherings would be greatly preferable than get-togethers every few generations.

Of people and time

If an annual cycle of inter-communal gatherings makes sense from a farming perspective, it also accords well with what we know about ancient views of time. Nowadays we have grown accustomed to a linear concept of time, in which we see our own time in terms of first prehistoric, then of historical development. So today, the day I am writing this passage (1 September 1997) can be seen as wholly different from the same date a year ago: the government has changed, Diana Princess of Wales died tragically yesterday and the world is grinding relentlessly towards the much-trumpeted Millennium. Modern time is linear and, it would sometimes seem, is becoming more so with each day that passes.

In the distant past, however, time was viewed as part of an endlessly repeated cycle, based on the seasons of the year. True, there was a linear element, centred on genealogy and tribal history, but that was not seen as part of the time-frame in which people actually lived and worked.

The 'real' farming world of tupping, of calving, of cultivation and of harvest was based on the seasons. In a way strange to modern patterns of thought, it did not matter that one particular year followed another: the cyclical view of time had more to do with order, organisation and preparedness than mere scheduling. We cannot, of course, be certain, but it is probable that the annual gatherings at Etton and sites like it would have been the climax of the farming and social year. In terms of the modern calendar, we would be thinking of Michaelmas or Lammas, at the earliest. By Christmas the weather would have clamped down and rising water levels would make travel difficult.

5 The longevity of landscapes

Of people, landscapes and families

We have already seen that divisions of some sort are needed, if conflicts between and within different farming communities are to be avoided. But this sounds rather arid: the layout of the landscape is about far more than just preventing possible disputes. The landscape is, after all, a place where people live out their lives. And of course there are landscapes within landscapes. A child will view the landscape very differently from an adult, just as a man will see it in a different way to a woman, or a priest to a farmer. I suspect that William Wordsworth saw the Lake District as a very different place to the men who ran their flocks across the Fells. But from a geographer's perspective the poet and the shepherd inhabited the same landscape.

So how would a prehistoric farmer have viewed the landscape? First and foremost, the farmer and his or her family would be steeped in the history of the countryside around them. We tend to think that in the remote past there was no history, as we know it today, because there was no writing. But in point of fact history was more personal — was probably more rich and diverse than the published local histories that are available to us today. The modern historian has to work from a relatively small number of published sources, but in prehistory every older person would carry in his or her head an account of the family and the land they farmed, that had been passed down from the previous generation. Nowadays we sit and watch television, listen to the radio and read newspapers, all of which talk of national affairs. In the past things were very different.

History today is a subject taught at school and essentially it is about 'them', not us. We rarely hear about the deeds of our own families, unless we happen to be Churchills, Darwins or Rothschilds. Local and family history has become a specialised topic and in my experience it is generally something people take to when they retire. In the past one's family history *was* general history, it included 'great' affairs of state — such as the conclusion of agreements with neighbouring tribes — and it also recalled the glorious deeds of previous generations — how great-great-grandfather won the duel which gave the family the woodland south of the river — or whatever.

Family history was a means of justifying and defining land tenure and it provided people with a clear idea of their own position within society — the rich man in his castle, the poor man at his gate. It was a topic which could not be escaped: every child would learn the family law. So it is manifestly absurd to suggest that there was no schooling in the remote past: there was plenty of it, but it took place at home, in the fields and perhaps after autumn suppers when the older people would recite verse or sing ballads about days long past.

To the prehistoric farmer and his or her family, the 'landscape of the mind', which added a living dimension to the landscape around them, would have been alive with the deeds of ancestors and great local heroes. Doubtless their spirits, good and bad, would have haunted various woods, marshes and lakes. But while this landscape of the mind had a life of its own, so to speak, it also had to exist alongside the day-to-day working landscape of the ordinary farmer. In fact the term 'working landscape' is very apt indeed: it was a place of work, but it also had itself to work, in the sense that a well-engineered machine 'works'. In other words, the various elements of the landscape combined together to form a coherent and well-organised system for the production of meat, milk, wool, grain, leather and other farm products.

As anyone knows who has had to buy a car, washing machine or anything that has to perform a useful function, it is always capable of improvement. By the same token, if circumstances change, then the machine may well have to be modified to make allowances for new conditions. Landscapes are like that too. In recent years the British countryside has changed faster and more radically than at any time in its history: in the 1960s and '70s trees were being felled, marshes drained and hedges were disappearing left and right to make spraying easier and to accommodate the new and ever-larger tractors. Then, by the mid-'80s the process slowed down a little and new planting of woodland and hedges began to be seen, as public opinion — and the grants that follow close behind — began to react against the prairie-like landscapes that other grants were helping to create. In the past the working landscape was prone to change too, but nobody in antiquity would have been stupid enough to put their own countryside through the frantic changes we have recently had to endure.

Working landscapes

In a working landscape farmers will see to it that their field boundary ditches are regularly cleaned-out and drystone walls repaired. Where I farm in the Fens, most dykes are mechanically re-dug about once every seven to ten years. All muck and silt — known by the splendid term 'slub' — is removed until the dyke looks fresh and clean. It makes little sense to stop the 'slubbing out' short of the bottom since the silt that has accumulated in the ditch is usually very soft and stagnant. This material is very loose and unstable. It is also an ideal growing medium, packed full of seeds and pieces of root which will quickly sprout into new plants. If the slub was not cleared thoroughly, reeds and rushes would rapidly re-choke the drain.

The same applies to ditches in less wet regions. Here the cleaning-out may happen once a generation, when the hedge around the field is re-laid and gaps are filled with new planting, but again, the digging out of the ditch will be thorough, else drainage will be impaired. And besides, most countrymen would not regard a poorly cleared-out ditch or badly laid hedge as 'a proper job', to use a popular Cornish phrase.

A ditch is one thing, but what about above ground features such as trees, walls and hedges? We will see in a subsequent chapter that is can be very difficult indeed to prove,

33   This hawthorn hedge had the misfortune to be in the path of a pipeline near Barnack, Cambridgeshire. It was probably planted in the early nineteenth century during the Enclosures. Note the difference of surface levels on either side. Also note that its roots barely penetrate into the underlying gravel sub-soil. In archaeological terms this hedge would leave almost no trace in the ground.

using conventional archaeological techniques, the existence of something as robust as an ancient hedgerow. Often the only clue to their existence is the ditch that *may* have run alongside them.

So if we are to grasp the true longevity of an ancient landscape we must think laterally, and this is something that modern archaeological recording systems do not encourage. The universally adopted recording system for excavations is one that was devised for deeply stratified urban excavations. It is based on vertical sections through accumulated layers of deposits, and on the way in which they built up, were removed, recut or whatever. When it works, as it usually does, it's very good; but its results can sometimes be very misleading, and it is at its worst when the method is applied to rural sites, and especially where working landscapes are involved. In these instances it will tend to ignore long periods when ditches, hedges and the like were subject to continous maintenance; sometimes centuries of work leave unsubstantial remains (**33, 34**). The end result is a picture of landscape development where only the very final stages — when the ditches were beginning to fill-in and where maintenance was failing — are recorded.

There are many reasons why it is difficult to estimate the age of a bygone landscape, but it *can* be done: it merely requires sustained effort, good luck and some lateral thinking. It

*34   The specialist in archaeological wood. Maisie Taylor ruefully considers a fine laid hedge in rural
Leicester. What archaeological trace would this superb example of the countryman's craft leave
for future generations? The answer is 'almost none'.*

also helps if one is not encumbered with a clumsy urban-style recording system. Of these factors, I think sustained effort is the most important: the more one works in any given region the more one develops a feel for what was going-on there. Lateral thinking is also very important and especially the way that landscape features, such as ditches respect the lie of the land. Is it, for example, entirely coincidental that a field boundary ditch dating seemingly to the Late Bronze Age is neatly lined-up on a barrow that was constructed a full millennium previously? In my experience, such 'coincidences' are rarely coincidental at all.

6 Slicing up the cake

Partitioning of the landscape: when did it start?

It has always struck me as both odd and ironic that one of the earliest-known field systems in northern Europe was found at the extreme edge of the Continent, at the point where the last, feeble ripples of the Neolithic 'wave of advance' merged with the rolling swell of the Atlantic Ocean. The fields in question were discovered and revealed by Dr Seamus Caulfield (of University College, Dublin) in County Mayo and they consist of neatly laid-out square and rectangular paddocks defined and enclosed by low drystone walls. The system is further divided up by double-ditched droveways and Dr Caulfield, whose family still farms in the region, is convinced that they were laid out and used for the management of livestock — particularly cattle. And I'm sure he is right.

The fields of Co. Mayo owe their survival to the blanketing effect of *Sphagnum* or moss peat which requires little to nourish it, other than rain. But apart from near-perfect preservation, what makes these fields so remarkable is their great antiquity: they have their origins in the fourth millennium BC and were used throughout the third. Can we match that in England? I only wish we could. At Fengate we have inklings of a very early organised landscape, but the evidence is very circumstantial indeed.

The hunt for the beginnings of landscape division (or land allotment, to use a term I prefer) began for me in 1972 during the second season of excavation at Fengate. As I recall, it had not been a particularly exciting year. We had excavated some very large areas indeed, but they revealed practically nothing and I was beginning to run out of money. I remember deciding to hire a small JCB digger to excavate part of a small field where cropmarks on air photos showed a few pits and hollows that looked to be man-made.

The digger worked away and, true to form that season, revealed nothing. I remember well the feeling of flatness and disappointment. It was depressing beyond belief and my crew were standing around, twiddling their thumbs and doing their best not to look resentful. They were mainly students from Canada and a very nice bunch. Anyhow, it had been a hot summer and the ground was dusty and dry. Under such conditions it is often very difficult to 'read' the stains and patches on the sub-soil surface so carefully exposed by the digger. Ditches show up as dark bands (**35**, **36**), post-holes as neat dark circles and pits as large, dark splodges — as if a giant had spilled brown ink on the ground. The different colours and textures are caused by the pit or ditch becoming filled with ancient topsoil that differs significantly from the parent subsoil or bedrock by virtue of being organic-rich and being filled with broken pottery, charcoal and other material. At Fengate

35   *This small Iron Age farming village at Fengate would rapidly have flooded had it not been criss-crossed by a network of drainange ditches which had to be kept open and in good repair. If one ditch blocked the entire system would begin to fail.*

the subsoil was gravel, but it had been churned about by the action of ice and meltwater during the last Ice Age; as a result it was not always very easy to distinguish between non-archaeological and man-made features.

An earlier Neolithic landscape at Fengate

As a general rule I have found that earlier archaeological features, such as Neolithic field boundary or barrow ditches, are usually much paler and harder to spot than, say, Roman or Iron Age features. Very often I suspect these elusive earlier features are missed by archaeologists not accustomed to gravel sites.

If a team of archaeological students has nothing to do, they will soon get fed-up, no matter how nice they might be. So I issued our team with onion hoes and we all began to scrape loose earth from the surfaces left by the digger. I was painfully aware that this was 'make work' but the soil was so dry that the digger had not been able to achieve a good surface, and much could lie hidden beneath all the loose material. That, at least, was the theory. And then it rained — not for long , maybe a quarter of an hour — and for a few fleeting minutes, before the ground became dry again, I saw the palest possible outline of a small square or rectangular building. The soil filling the foundation trenches was very pale indeed — which suggested an early date.

36   *Bronze Age droveway ditches during excavation at Fengate, July 1974. Behind the two teams of archaeologists can be seen the dark marks of the unexcavated ditches which contrast with the paler colours of the natural gravel subsoil.*

It took us several weeks to excavate the building and in the process we discovered a fine collection of flint tools and pottery together with some rather more exotic finds. These included a deliberately struck flake from off a polished stone axes made from stone quarried at Langdale in Cumbria, and a large, highly polished jet bead of a type usually found in burials. Twelve years later our excavation at Etton produced many deliberately struck flakes that had been removed from polished stone axes. We did not recognise it then, but we had found evidence for the ritualised destruction of a valuable and highly cherished artefact. By the end of the season the team's usually high morale had returned — and I could relax.

In those days I operated from the Royal Ontario Museum in Toronto who were joint sponsors of the excavation, together with the old Department of Public Buildings and Works (now, after several changes of identity, English Heritage). Back in my office in Toronto I pored over the plans and sections we had drawn in the field and spent many days sifting through the excellent selection of British archaeological journals in the University library. There was no escaping it: we had excavated what was probably the earliest house then known in England. Subsequently it has become clear that the 'house' was not a building for the living, but somewhere for the dead (hence the jet bead and the smashed axe).

I didn't realise it then, but the discovery of the Fengate 'house' was the first piece in a jigsaw puzzle that might hold the clues to the shape — or rather the merest outline — of

37   *Excavations at Fengate in 1972 revealed two parallel ditches that had been cut into limestone. It is probable that together they formed a narrow droveway of probable Neolithic date (c2000-2500 BC). The droveways at Fengate were intended to confine livestock to a narrow strip of land, so as to cause the minimum disturbance and disruption to animals in surrounding fields.*

a very early landscape indeed. The second clue was revealed in 1975, but several hundred metres away from the 'house'. It was far less exciting and merely consisted of two parallel ditches, perhaps forming the sides of a track or droveway (**37**). These ditches were cut into limestone at a point where the gravel subsoil had thinned-out. Even though there were several Iron Age pits, post-holes and other domestic features in the immediate vicinity, the two ditches produced no finds, apart from a fragment of Langdale polished stone axe — just like the one from the 'house'. At the time I was struck by the fact that the ditches did not produce any Iron Age pottery which was very abundant indeed elsewhere, and I concluded — correctly I believe — that the ditches and the 'house' were Neolithic and broadly contemporary.

The trail then went quiet for two years while we concentrated our efforts on the Bronze Age fields which I will discuss in subsequent chapters. Then in 1975 we discovered a most remarkable burial, about 150m north-east of the 'house'. The burial seems to have been that of a complete family. There were four bodies: an adult man, aged 25-30 years, a woman of about the same age, a toddler aged 3-4 and a child aged 8-12. All were buried together in a large pit. The dating evidence consisted of a single leaf-shaped flint

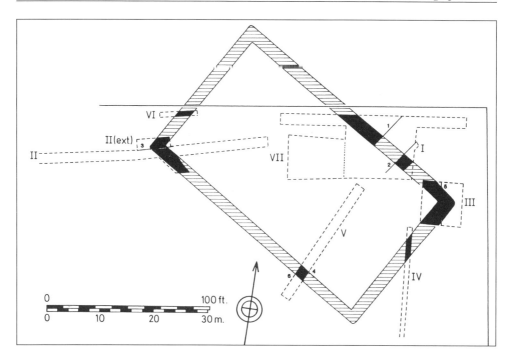

38   *Plan of a rectangular enclosure excavated at Fengate in 1969. It was once thought that this enclosure was domestic and of Early Bronze Age (Beaker) date, but it is now recognised that it was probably a Neolithic mortuary enclosure — a special area laid aside for the dead.*

arrowhead which was found lodged between the man's eighth and ninth ribs. Presumably the arrowhead caused the man's death, but whether directly or through subsequent infection is hard to determine. Leaf-shaped arrowheads of that particular type belong within the Neolithic period.

The next development in the story happened very much later when I had completed the main Fengate reports and was writing-up for English Heritage an excavation that had taken place at Fengate in 1969, three years before I began my own project there. The site in question (known as Site 11) had always been a puzzle (**38**). It consisted of a very neatly laid-out rectangular enclosure, roughly half the size of a tennis court. Within it there was a post-built roundhouse, but I was able to demonstrate that this was about a millennium later than the enclosure and belonged with the subsequent Bronze Age field system (which I'll discuss shortly). So what purpose did the enclosure serve, if not to surround a house?

And now for an extraordinary coincidence. While I was working on the publication of Site 11, I happened to be staying with my friend and colleague Dr Ian Kinnes. Ian is a foremost scholar of the Neolithic and at the time we were busy working through some of the finds from Etton which are now at the British Museum. One evening I casually mentioned Site 11, as one does, and Ian replied to my surprise that he had been the supervisor there, while still a student at Cambridge. Of course I should have recognised his distinctive writing in the notebooks, but I didn't. Anyhow, I told him what I thought about the dating of the roundhouse and how that left the neatly laid-out enclosure on its own — high and dry.

I remember Ian's reply as if it were yesterday: 'Oh, no, it doesn't,' he said, 'quite the opposite. That house was always the problem. Take the house away and you're left with a mortuary enclosure — like the ones that turned up the other day on air photos in Essex.' I knew the ones he meant. They were Neolithic all right.

As soon as I got home I laid out the Fengate plans on the floor and it all fell into place: the little rectangular 'house' with the axe fragment and the jet bead was on precisely the same alignment as the newly recognised mortuary enclosure. They simply *had* to go together! Then I noticed something else, potentially far more important.

The parallel ditches that we had found the year we excavated the little rectangular 'house' were also aligned in the same direction as the other two Neolithic features — not only that, but the long axis of the mortuary enclosure pointed pretty well directly at the big grave with the family burial.

The latest twist in the tale happened earlier this summer (July 1997) when a team from the Cambridge University Unit was excavating a site in Fengate as part of a commercial Planning Application contract. They were working just over 500m south-east of the initial Neolithic discoveries when they came across yet another Neolithic mortuary structure, with pottery identical to that found in the original house-that-wasn't. This new structure was built using post-holes, rather than trenches, but in general size and layout it was similar to the 1972 'house'. Most importantly of all — at least for the present story — it appeared to be orientated on the same NE-SW alignment as the other four features. So what does this tale of alignments tell us?

The axis of the landscape

One does not need to be a geographer to realise that the shape of the landscape reflects the lie of the land. As one flies over England, the wide, flat lowland valleys below are covered by large rectangular fields and the roads are generally straight or gently curving. When the ground starts to rise the fields become smaller and the roads more sinuous. But these are just the most obvious differences. If we land our plane and walk through the countryside it soon becomes apparent that the folk who set out the fields we are walking through knew exactly what they were doing. They understood the almost infinite subtleties behind that old phrase 'the lie of the land'.

The positioning of fields and roadways, of houses and yards does not just respect the rise and fall of the ground, but also its drainage, shelter, shade and soil type. I am always amazed by the extraordinarily detailed mental map that most farmers carry around in their heads — and not just of their own land, but that of their friends, neighbours and relations too. When I bought the land I now farm, a good half dozen people warned me about a damp patch in the north-east corner of the northernmost field and the persistent blackgrass along the eastern headland; most were aware that about half of the old clay land drain pipes had become blocked — and they were kind enough to say so.

One might have thought that a landscape as flat as the Fens was so lacking in features that fields could be laid-out more or less at random — simply to suit the needs of the farmer. But nothing could be further from the truth. When the land is flat — or nearly so (I know of no absolutely flat land in the Fens) — the slight slopes that remain become of crucial importance, for how else is water to be removed? Only a fool would dig a drainage dyke at the foot of a slope, even if the slope had a gradient of 20cm in 500m. Water can only flow downhill.

In many instances fields may be laid out with regard to the quality of the soil within them. Where I farm it is quite common to find fields with a 'good' and a 'bad' end — the 'good' being freely draining silt and the 'bad' heavy clay. Sometimes entire fields are 'good' or 'bad'. And of course 'bad' for one person is 'good' for another. My land is 'bad' for growing potatoes, but being heavy it is very good for growing grass. Clay retains moisture well, so our grass generally manages to stay good and green during the drought summers that seem to be so common these days.

In areas like the Fens, the Fen margins and lowland river valley floodplains, land was generally divided-up in such a way that each farmer had several types of land in his holding. In other words it made little sense for one person to own all the floodplain grazing while another owned all the flood-free land around the edges. If that happened the floodplain farmer would have nowhere to move his stock during the winter floods and the man at the edge would be short of grass when the summer sun scorched his freely-draining grazing land. So the wetter ground and the land around it was divided-up into holdings which radiated out from the wetland, more of less at right-angles to it.

This pattern of land allotment led to a ladder-like arrangement of fields along the Fen-edge plain of Lincolnshire, for example. Smaller patches of marsh or fen would look more like a huge darts board with the wet marshy bit as the bull's eye, and fields radiating around it. Farmers around the edges of the Fen and smaller wetlands would often hold the wetland in common; this would give them rights to graze stock and take hay and sometimes peat too at the appropriate times of the year. Similar arrangements still apply in upland areas, where farmers below the high heather moorland have rights to run their sheep on the open moor from spring to autumn.

The mixing-up and muddling together of stock on common grazing can be a potential source of friction between farmers. Today moorland sheep are marked and ear-tagged and allowed to run free. In the past sheep in the common pastures would often have been tended either by professional shepherds or in remoter periods by children, relatives and perhaps the farmer as well. To get the herds and flocks from the fields to the common pasture the farmers constructed droveways which followed the layout of the fields and ran at right-angles to the common grazing.

The droveways also served to separate the individual holdings of land and it is quite possible that some prehistoric droveways, for example those at West Deeping, in southern Lincolnshire, which I will discuss shortly, were actually the property of individual farmers or farming families. We will see shortly that many droveways were boundaries as well as roadways, and they were an essential component of landscapes that were farmed for livestock. So how did the orientation of the very ancient, earlier Neolithic, landscape at Fengate reflect or follow the lie of the land, and to what extent did it obey the rules I have just sketched out?

The lie of the land

As a rule, the 'lie of the land' — defined in its broadest sense — will be the main factor behind the arrangement of a farmed landscape. So one can predict, in the most general terms, more or less how a field system will be aligned if one knows the contours of the land, the river or drainage pattern and the underlying geology. But one encounters problems when contours, rivers and the subtleties of the underlying geology are hidden beneath peats and alluvium. And that is precisely what happened at Fengate. We were prevented from relating features in the landscape to the countryside itself. It was bizarre — so we had to turn the usual way of doing things on its head; this meant we had to predict the shape of the Neolithic landscape from the orientation of man-made features upon it. It was like trying to map the course of the Thames from the arrangement of streets around Tower Hill.

Now when we plotted the orientation of the earlier Neolithic features it was apparent that they must have been laid out in an organised landscape, for which there is very little archaeological evidence. Perhaps this landscape was parcelled-up with hedges that have left no trace. I cannot be certain, but it would seem very likely. The alignment of the four (now five) Neolithic features is significantly different from that of the large Bronze Age field system that followed, but it is not radically different — a matter of some twenty degrees, no more (**39**). Of course it is pure speculation, but the Neolithic alignment would fit better if the landscape were focused upon a stream, known as the Cat's Water which flows along the Fen-edge at this point. The alignment of this very early landscape does not fit well with the edge of the fen proper and some major adjustments would have been needed in later Bronze Age times, had the Neolithic system survived that long.

We know from radiocarbon dates taken from deeply buried peats that the fen at Fengate did not begin to form until about 2000 BC — so it would make perfect sense to align the Neolithic landscape on a stream, and not on a fen which had yet to happen! As to the date of this early landscape, one can only hazard a rough guess — maybe 3500-2500 BC?

Alas, archaeology is never straightforward. Recent work has shown that the edge of the fen on which the earlier Neolithic landscape was aligned may well have been wet well before 2000 BC. It has also shown that the very edge of the wet ground was inhabited in the earlier Neolithic period. In the face of the new evidence I am coming to the view that the earliest landscape may well have been a ribbon or strip of cleared ground — and not an open space within the woods. Perhaps the actual route that people used to drive their animals to and from the fens, from higher ground to the west, may have been the starting point for what was later to evolve into an organised landscape. As an idea I think it would make more practical sense than merely making random clearings in the forest — of no particular shape. I suspect this principle will apply in other parts of the country, too.

So those are the hints of an earlier Neolithic organised landscape at Fengate, and on the whole I think they are quite convincing. But how did it end, and what was happening elsewhere in the region at the time?

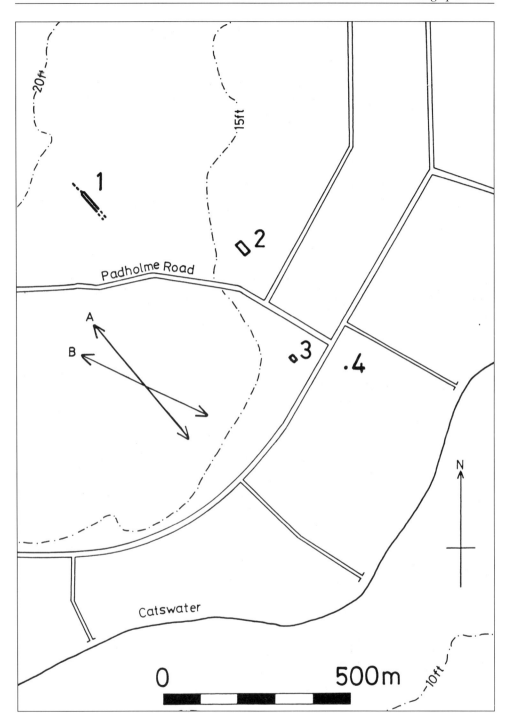

39   *A map showing the orientation of two Fengate landscapes: Neolithic (arrow A) and Bronze Age (arrow B). The fragmentary components of the Neolithic landscape are shown by numbers, thus: 1 (droveway ditches), 2 (mortuary structure), 3 ('house') and 4 (multiple burial).*

Homes, fields and gardens

Now there are very few *bona fide* field systems from the earlier Neolithic period. This rarity or absence might reflect our inability to recognise them, or it may be caused by the fact that they used hedges without ditches. It is also possible that the very earliest field boundaries were removed by later fields. But a simpler explanation may also be possible: they are extremely rare because they *were* extremely rare. I don't think that this is as odd as it might at first appear.

We have grown accustomed to our own landscape and we unconsciously impose our ways of doing things on past cultures. We are used to a landscape of fields. And in the fields we grow crops and we keep animals. The fields provide containment and protection to both. So we can walk away and leave them — crops and stock — alone and untended, in the certain knowledge that they will be safe. But was it always possible to behave like that? To take the argument a step further, why and when did it become necessary to have fields at all?

I will consider the way that crops were grown when I write about the 'dark earth' at Welland Bank, but I am convinced that in the Neolithic and Bronze Age most cereal crops were grown in gardens, in plots very close to the settlement. They were not grown in the open countryside in fields. Today when we think about wheat and barley we imagine the huge fields of East Anglia — rolling acres and not a weed in sight. But it has been experimentally demonstrated that in prehistory the crop would have been choked with weeds and I would imagine that such a mass of vegetation would be very prone indeed to storm and rain damage; it would make far more practical sense to have it growing close to the settlement and in a sheltered spot where people could keep a close eye on it. Cereals grow just as well in gardens as they do in open fields.

I remember being most forcibly struck by the closeness of the cereal plots to the domestic and farm buildings when I first visited the Little Butser experimental Iron Age farm in Hampshire. My guide explained that they didn't have the land to plants the crops in fields away from the settlement, but at the time I remember thinking, why bother? Why not keep them close to where the farmer lived, as this was both secure and handy when it came to spreading manure.

Divide and rule

Now animals only have to be kept in fields when their population (and perhaps that of their owners too) reaches a point where the available grazing needs to be managed with greater control. Archaeologists tend to forget that fields are just as important for keeping animals *out* as they are for keeping animals *in*. The academic literature on early animal husbandry is full of dire warnings about wild animals entering the stockyards and the importance of excluding wild genes from the domestic herd — wild boar and wild cattle (aurochs) being the two obvious examples in northern Europe. Whether or not one could exclude a sex-mad, rampaging aurochs or wild boar from a domestic corral by a field or yard boundary fence is something I would love to see being tested by experiment. And I would also like to examine the physical state and mental condition of the experimenters afterwards! Surely the wise stockman would have seen to it that most wild males in the surrounding forest were eliminated well in advance of the domestic females coming into season; or else he would know tricks to divert them from his farm at that crucial time. No, it was not the keeping out of wild animals that I was thinking about.

Simply by excluding stock, field boundaries will allow over-grazed areas of grass to recover; they will also give dung lying on the surface a chance to break-down and become incorporated into the turf. At a microscopic level, periodic breaks in grazing allow a degree of control of the internal parasites (nematodes, fluke and other horrors) which would otherwise become a very serious problem indeed. Such means of control are not necessary when the pressure on grazing is slight. In circumstances of under- or low population, the stock can perfectly well be controlled by children or adults who simply live with and follow the animals wherever they go. In some of these systems of extensive management there may be very little need actually to control where the beasts wander; in others the control exerted may be considerable. It depends on the quality of grazing and, of course, on the population of livestock.

I suspect, but cannot yet prove, that the countryside around and about Etton in the early fourth millennium BC would have been managed extensively, with livestock from each community wandering through its own area of cleared woodland. Each family would have herded its own flock and it would have been rare for animals to wander off into the territory of neighbouring communities. Then, as time passed and populations rose, the woods were progressively pushed back and clearings coalesced to form tracts of open countryside, so the need for some other type of boundary to replace the felled forest began to arise. Causewayed enclosures, such as Etton, formed a focus for the ceremonial and social life of the community, but they were not necessarily positioned at the centre of any particular community's territory. In fact I suspect that, being places where people met regularly, they may well have been located on the boundaries between two or more communities.

If something as large as a causewayed enclosure could mark out part of a boundary or frontier, then it perhaps follows that the earliest tribal or community frontiers, following the widespread clearance of the natural forest, were marked out by substantial monuments such as the great 'cursus' which runs diagonally across Maxey 'island' or the double-ditched henge complex on the south side of the 'island'.

Some henge-like sites can be seen on air photos of Maxey to cluster together into groups, others stand on their own, in splendid isolation. This would suggest that henges were horses-for-courses: some were prominent markers of something or somewhere important (such as the corner of a territory or frontier), whereas others may have been little more than small family shrines. But whatever their actual use, henges and other ring-ditch sites start to proliferate across the landscape at the time when forest clearance is beginning to make major advances. As sites in their own right, they would have made little impact in woodland: a circle of posts in a forest of tall trees makes little sense. But viewed across a grassy plain and surrounded by a bank and ditch in freshly exposed white limestone gravel, they would have been spectacular indeed.

The absence of field boundaries from the landscape around these Late Neolithic sites could be explained as 'archaeological invisibility' — in other words they used unmarked

*40   After nearly four millennia of ploughing and farming, the mound within the circular quarry
       ditch of this Early Bronze Age barrow at Fengate has disappeared. But it must once have been
       a striking feature in the landscape, as the Bronze Age field boundary ditches alongside it were
       probably laid out using the barrow as a marker.*

hedges. But I can see no reason why we should attempt such special pleading — after all
hedges work and can be established very much better if they are accompanied by a ditch
and bank of some sort.

In my experience hedges are rarely found without some sort of earthwork marker,
however small. No, the simplest explanation is that in the centuries between the
widespread clearance of the forest cover and the construction of the earliest known fields
— around 1600-1800 BC — the landscape was divided up using a system of marker points
which could have been monuments, such as henges or barrows, or equally something less
permanent, like large oak trees, streams and so on. Streams and rivers have always been
important natural boundaries and trees were commonly used as such in Saxon times. The
main frontiers would be the earliest and most important and these would have been
between different communities; then, as time passed and the pressure on land grew, the
communal territory would have become sub-divided into smaller, perhaps family-based,
territories or holdings.

After 2000 BC at the onset of the Early Bronze Age we find large numbers of round
barrows appearing across the landscape. These burial mounds were also territorial markers
— again it would seem reasonable to suppose they marked out family holdings — and in
many instances we find that the earliest field boundary ditches are either aligned on them,
or respect them in some way. At West Deeping (as we shall see shortly) and Fengate (**40**)

the Early Bronze Age round barrows and ring-ditches appear to be spread quite evenly through the later field systems, as if they formed a basis for their arrangement. It's rather as if the later fields were 'pegged out' on a framework provided by the slightly earlier barrows.

I find it very interesting that the Bronze Age field systems extend around and between the barrows. This would suggest that the landscape in the area had always been used for the running of stock and that the barrows had never sat in isolated splendour within their own deserted 'ritual landscape'. Instead of robed Druid-like priests intoning mystical incantations as the fen mists rolled across a depopulated landscape, we must imagine open or scrubby country with numerous small flocks of small brown sheep and long-horned cattle, tended by men with dogs and children with sticks. I would imagine that people, old and young, treated the barrows with enormous respect — for that is where their ancestors now resided — but otherwise the landscape was what it had always been — a place where people lived and animals fed.

Our story has now passed the year 2000 BC and we find ourselves in the Early Bronze Age. We have seen how the open countryside was divided up, following the clearance of the Neolithic woods, and we have seen how it may have been farmed. It is now time to shift up a gear — to move from a system of extensive farming to something much more familiar. It is three thousand, seven hundred years ago, and I would imagine that even then some worthy people are beginning to complain about the intensive new methods of farming: those new-fangled fields, those walls, those ditches, they're so horribly cruel — why can't sheep wander through the woods in small flocks, tended by a small boy with a pointed stick — as nature intended?

Of winter hardwood cuttings

We have already discussed boundaries and the need for them at some length, but now I want to address a simpler, more nitty-gritty question, because it has wider and important implications: we have seen that in large areas of lowland Britain the land was probably divided-up by hedges, but how did ancient people plant and maintain them? Were they capable of such a thing?

When one sees maps or plans of prehistoric fields in archaeological reports and textbooks they look at first glance very convincing. But then one looks more closely at the scale and one realises that ditches that were supposed to keep animals within a field or farmyard were extremely shallow — maybe a couple of feet (say half-a-metre) deep. Sometimes they were half that depth. Such a ditch on its own wouldn't deter a vole, let alone a sexed-up ram in search of female companionship. So how did they work?

The answer to this question lies not in the little ditch but in what ran alongside it, namely the bank (**41**). The ditch was dug not to be a boundary in itself, but to provide a bank. It is true that together a ditch and bank form a more substantial earthwork than either on their own, alone, as the builders of hillforts and castles knew only too well. But frankly a half-metre deep ditch and a bank of about the same height scarcely constitutes an obstacle to even a newly born lamb. No, I am quite convinced that the purpose of the bank was quite different, and relatively short-lived.

41   *The archaeologist Chris Evans stands in a Bronze Age field boundary ditch at Fengate, 1978.*
To Chris' right is a low bank that probably supported a hedge; without a hedge, the small ditch
and bank could not possibly be stock-proof by themselves.

I have been a keen gardener all of my life and I get special pleasure from producing my own plants. There are a number of propagation methods which are of varying effectiveness, depending on the plant one is trying to reproduce. Some are vegetative techniques, such as stem or leaf cuttings, layering etc. that involve the removal of plant tissue, rather than the setting of seeds. In other instances it is simpler to collect and sow seeds. It's a case of horses-for-courses: one selects the propagation method that suits the growing conditions and the plant one is attempting to reproduce.

The main drawback with sowing seeds is that mice and other small animals — especially in an open growing ground — will eat them and germination can be, at best, unreliable. Seeds, for example sloes and hazel nuts, are best grown in protected surroundings and the seedlings are then pricked out, the following autumn or spring, into their permanent position.

Cuttings can be more straightforward, particularly if the cutting material carries its own built-in defences in the form of thorns. Cuttings that involve green or semi-ripe material are not suitable for the setting of hedges, as they require too much protection from sunlight and wind — being very prone to drying-out. But by far and away the best method of planting hedges, especially stock-proof thorn hedges, is to strike winter hardwood cuttings. It's very simple: in late autumn one takes cuttings from the growth of the summer that has just finished. The wood must be woody and fully ripe and the ground into which the cuttings are pushed must be loose and free-draining. Rot is the great enemy of cuttings and they must never become waterlogged. Hawthorn, sloe and dog rose root very readily from hardwood cuttings and will form an impenetrable hedge, depending on ground conditions, in about five years.

A freshly cast-up bank and ditch make an ideal planting medium for a winter hardwood cutting hedge, even in heavy clay land. The friable, humic topsoil from the ditch is placed on one side to form a bank. After one or two frosts even the clay clods of the bank will break up, to form an ideal rooting medium. On lighter sub-soils such as sand and gravel it may not even be necessary to dig a ditch, but cuttings are always vulnerable to casual damage and a small marking-out ditch or bank might help to avoid such problems.

The cuttings then sit dormant all winter and in spring the buds burst and roots sprout from around the base. Providing the spring is not too dry and windy — as the young newly rooted cuttings are quite vulnerable to drying-out — the hedge will be recognisable as such the following autumn.

Winter hardwood cuttings were used to plant the hedges along the roadsides of the many new Enclosure Act roads of the early nineteenth century and local woodland was used as the source for the parent material. That is why our older hedges retain such a rich source of intra-species diversity, despite the fact that many of the original woods which provided the source material for the cuttings have long since vanished. Nobody knows when the taking of winter hardwood cuttings began, but it is such a very basic technique that it is hard to believe it never existed.

7 Old straight tracks

Poring over pictures

My first major excavation was at Fengate, an industrial suburb on the eastern outskirts of Peterborough. The site was already well-known to prehistorians, so I knew I had something solid to get my teeth into. In addition to the work of various distinguished scholars in the first four decades of the century, the site had benefited enormously from a detailed survey carried out by Chris Taylor of the Royal Commission on Historical Monuments. Chris revealed to a wider archaeological audience a series of remarkable air photos taken in the 1950s by the justly famous Cambridge aerial archaeologist, Professor J K St Joseph (known affectionately to all as 'Holy Joe'). Holy Joe's photos showed the Fengate landscape to be traversed by a series of paired straight cropmark ditches, which Chris Taylor, rightly as it turned out, thought were trackways.

I got hold of as many Holy Joe pictures as I could find, and pored over them with the largest magnifying glass I could borrow. As I peered at the photos I began to discern more, very faint, double-ditched trackways. It took me some time to transcribe the cropmarks from oblique photos to a map (**42**), but as I worked it soon became apparent that the tracks were straight, parallel and very carefully laid-out. I was looking at a system, but what on earth, I thought, are a series of parallel tracks doing on the edge of the Fens?

It took us four years — between 1971 and 1974 — to answer that question. During that time our team carried out a series of increasingly large-scale excavations that proved that the trackways were in fact specialised droveways for livestock (**43**). They formed the main elements of a large field system that was laid out along the edge of the Fen and at right angles to the wetlands, at some time in the earlier Bronze Age (**44**). Radiocarbon dates now suggest that this happened around, or shortly after, 1800 BC. This highly organised Bronze Age landscape continued to be used and to 'work' until about 900 BC when it was replaced by another, seemingly less tightly organised landscape, which probably lasted throughout the Iron Age and into the Roman period. Sometime after the third century AD this later landscape was abandoned, in the face of continued and widespread flooding.

The Bronze Age landscape at Fengate was a very specialised one: designed for the management of large numbers of animals. The subsequent Iron Age landscape was laid out and used at a time when the nearby fen was very wet and may not have been available as a source of summer grazing. Maybe that is why the wide droveway that led into the Iron Age farm was not aligned on the fen at all — in fact it points inland, almost in the opposite direction. It's as if the prehistoric farmers are trying to send us a very direct message!

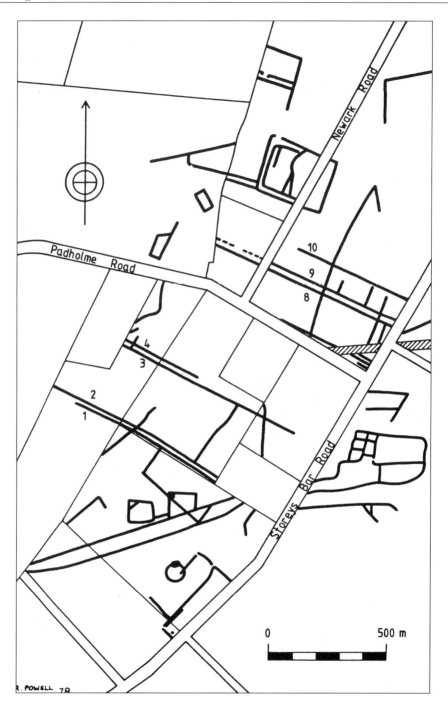

42   *Cropmarks on aerial photographs of Fengate were transcribed onto maps. This shows the main, numbered (1-10) ditches of a Bronze Age field system, together with an Iron Age and Romano-British droveway leading into farmyards on either side of Storey's Bar Road. Note how the two sets of cropmarks are laid-out on different alignments.*

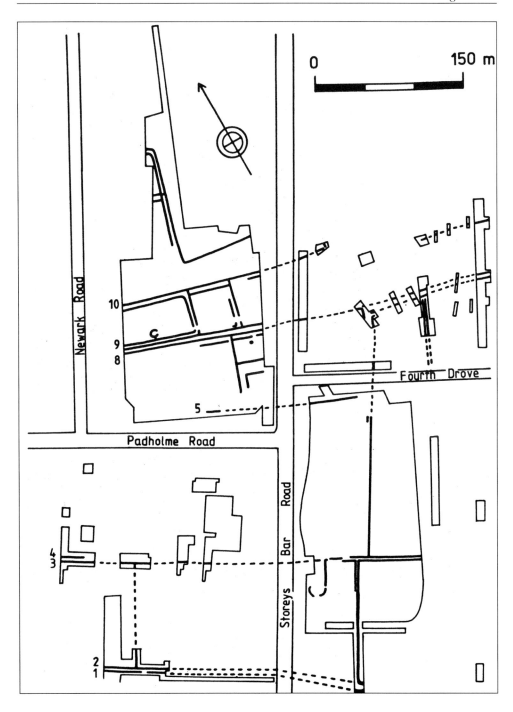

43   The Fengate Bronze Age cropmarks were excavated between 1971 and 1978 and were clearly seen to form part of a well laid-out, coherent system of fields, paddocks and droveways.

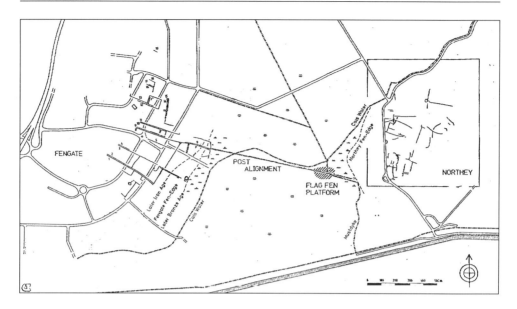

44   *Twenty years after the main Fengate campaign of 1971-78, continuing research has demonstrated that the original Bronze Age ditched fields and droveways formed part of a coherent landscape arranged on either side of, and probably all around, the Flag Fen basin.*

Anyhow, all the evidence suggests that the Iron Age landscape revolved around mixed farming in which livestock and cereal agriculture were both important. That, in the briefest posible outline, is the prehistory of the Fengate landscape.

Ideas, theories and hypotheses

Good archaeology is structured archaeology. Anyone who seriously believes that excavation does not require a great deal of forethought is a fool. I remember having a blazing row with an incompetent supervisor who yelled at me in a tumult of fury: 'the trouble with you is you have ...' — then he groped for words, '... *preconceived ideas!*' He was right, of course, I do. But there is a very big difference between having an open mind and an empty mind.

When I started work at Fengate in 1971 I brought with me a small team from Canada, and I also took on students from one or two English universities. We worked away quietly and I was very aware that I was finding my archaeological feet. I don't think we made very much of an impression at all within the wider British archaeological community after our first two seasons' work. Then late in 1972 the dig was visited by a young, bespectacled Cambridge academic with unfashionably short hair and a big grin. David Clarke was the very last person I would have expected to turn up on site. Sadly he is no longer with us, but at the time he was a leading theoretician — indeed he almost single-handed invented archaeological theory in Britain.

I showed David around the dig and he was most attentive and asked searching questions

— which in retrospect I answered very inadequately. Anyhow, a few weeks later he invited me round to his rooms in Peterhouse.

When I arrived, I knocked at the door and found him on his hands and knees on the carpet surrounded by blow-up photocopies of the site plans of the Glastonbury Lake Village. Over tea we talked at length about wetlands and the way people exploited them in the past. He taught me about the importance of looking into the medieval and recent history of the place and showed how the relationship of the wetland and dryland was never static — it changed with the year and the season.

I drove back to Peterborough with my head buzzing. It had been a crucial meeting: after that visit to David Clarke I could never see our fields and droveways as things that existed on their own, in isolation as it were. I had to try and work out how the landscape, of which they formed a key part, worked. And to do that I had to think about other landscapes in the region. As David put it — and he was heavily into Systems Theory at the time — I had to consider how the various landscape systems interacted and changed through time. It was a daunting prospect, even when I had cut my way through the jargon, but I had a pretty clear idea where I had to start my quest: common-sense dictated that the Fens *had* to have played an important role in determining what happened around their margins.

The following winter I returned to Canada and there had a remarkable bit of luck. Within the University of Toronto is the Pontifical Institute for Mediaeval Studies and within that Institute was a most remarkable scholar, Father J Ambrose Raftis, who had made a speciality of the history — and most particularly the economic and agrarian history — of Fenland religious houses and the villages around them. Father Raftis was advising our animal bones specialist, Kathy Biddick, who was using the Fengate bones as a major part of her PhD thesis. David Clarke had stressed to me the importance of looking at medieval patterns of life, and now from the other side of the Atlantic my attention was being focused on matters medieval by two very strong personalities. It was almost enough to make one believe that there was a destiny that shaped one's ends. At all events I read quite deeply in the subject and have kept an eye — albeit very much an amateur's eye — on the medieval Fens ever since.

Structured mobility

My reading in the history of the medieval Fenland led me to realise that the crucial concept behind the prehistoric exploitation of the Fen-edge landscape was mobility, but it was not random mobility. It was structured mobility within clearly defined limits, and the intention was to avoid disputes with neighbouring farmers and more distant communities, and also to manage finite reserves of hay and grazing efficiently.

The pattern of movement was simple: in wintertime the entire community stayed on the higher, flood-free land of the Fen-edge. So far as we can tell, Bronze Age farmers at Fengate lived in small farms consisting of a single round house and perhaps an outbuilding or two. These farms were spread through the field system and rarely showed much evidence for rebuilding. This might suggest that they were built by a family for their own use and probably lasted no more than a generation apiece. So in winter I suspect the houses would have been hives of activity, with the whole family present. When water levels in the nearby fen began to fall, perhaps in late April or May, a part of the community would head out into the open fen pastures together with most of the sheep and lambs, cows and calves. These animals would perhaps be tended by the older children of the family under the supervision of an adult or two.

The family would be re-united in the autumn when the water levels began to rise, perhaps in October or November. With fattened lambs and fatted calves this would be the time for festivals and celebration; this would also be the time of the Autumn Fair, when old beasts were culled and when livestock was exchanged between different families.

The Bronze Age landscape at Fengate was divided up into a series of blocks or parcels of land, by ditched droveways which ran down to the wetter land at right-angles, in the approved medieval manner, with each farmer having some higher land, some occasionally flooded land, and some wetland.

This theoretical interpretation of the way the Bronze Age landscape was managed was fine, so far as it went, and most of my colleagues were convinced, but I still wanted to prove it, if at all possible. I reckoned that the best proof would lie at the end of a droveway, at the point where the dryland met the wet.

Unfortunately we never managed to get close enough to the wetland edge, during the main Fengate campaign of 1971-78, but in 1989 the construction of a new power station gave us an ideal opportunity. We mechanically stripped and excavated a huge area ahead of the power station's construction and found two droveway ditches which ran east towards the wetter land. And then, to our great delight, right on the very edge of the wet, the ditches veered sharply away in opposite directions and ran north and south along the boundary between wet and dry (**45**). But the 'mouth' of the droveway opened directly onto the open fen pastures of the Flag Fen basin. There could be no doubt about its original function: it was intended to bring livestock to and from the Fen. It was obviously a particularly important droveway as its side ditches (ditches 8 and 9 of the original system) were very large indeed. For convenience I will refer to it as the Main Drove (**col. pl. 1-4**). We will see shortly that some of the droveways of the Borough Fen Bronze Age field system behave in precisely the same way when they too meet the edge of the wet.

The Main Drove was undoubtedly a very important boundary within the field system and I would venture to suggest that this was just as important as its droving role.

Now when we first revealed the layout and extent of the Fengate Bronze Age fields to a rather sceptical archaeological world, back in 1973, many colleagues thought that our 'droveways' could have been the result of field enlargement. I thought then (and still think now) that this was a ludicrous suggestion. What they are saying is that the Bronze Age farmer first decides to make his fields bigger by a mere two or three metres. Then he makes up his mind to do it in the most time-consuming and labour-intensive way imaginable — by ripping up an established hedge. To do that for so small a gain of land, is manifestly absurd. But on the other hand there is no persuading some people, so we decided to do a soil phosphate survey within and around the Main Drove, in the hope that it would provide us with a new strand of independent, objective information. As we saw at Etton, soil phosphate analysis can reveal areas where manure was applied, or stored, or just accumulated. Think of it as an archaeological muck-detector.

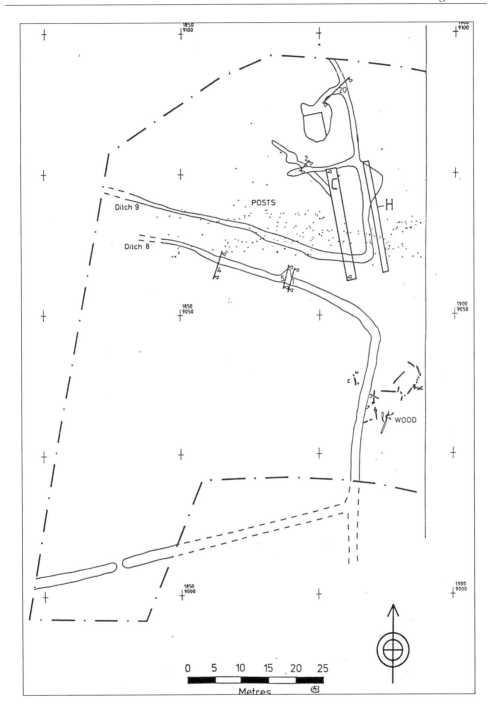

Ditch 9

Ditch 8

POSTS

WOOD

0   5   10   15   20   25

Metres

45   At the point where the Bronze Age droveway (defined by ditches 8 and 9) met the wetland of
      Flag Fen, the side ditches opened out and headed north and south along the fen margins.
      Animals driven along the drove from higher ground to the west would now be free to spread
      over the rich pasture of the open fen.

A prehistoric 'piss-mire'

The Fengate phosphate survey was one of the first large-scale surveys of its kind and we turned to the only institution with sufficient experience of such a project for help — The British Museum. Dr Paul Craddock of their Research Laboratory helped us design the project and he also helped us set up a small laboratory on site. He was extraordinarily helpful in other ways too, and arranged for a team of trainees from North Sea Camp, a Detention Centre on the Wash coast near Boston, to come and work on the excavations; whether such a thing would be permitted in these unenlightened days of the Short Sharp Shock is, however, open to doubt. When not working on phosphates, Paul and I would indulge in his second great interest — medieval churches. Armed with a copy of 'St Nick' (the relevant county in Pevsner's monumental *The Buildings of England*), we would visit the magnificent parish churches of Fenland and Paul would painstakingly deconstruct the various phases of their complex construction; completely wrapped-up in his thoughts, I frequently had to guide him around ecclesiastical obstacles, such as pews, pulpits and old ladies arranging flowers. We could usually — no, invariably — be found in the local pub at the conclusion of the day's churchifying.

The results of Paul's phosphate survey showed beyond doubt that the surface of the Main Drove had been used by livestock and in such numbers that the grass had been worn away allowing the phosphate to 'lock' into the underlying topsoil. In the scientific report Paul used a splendid Cornish phrase to describe prehistoric surface conditions: a 'piss-mire'. We were later to realise that the 'piss-mire' was not caused by normal farm traffic, but by very large numbers of animals indeed. Closer to the edge of the wetland at the very end of the Main Drove we found evidence for trampling, in the form of rather indistinct and disturbed animal hoof-marks, which were sealed beneath the overlying layers of alluvium. It's difficult to be certain whether the animal trample is Bronze or Iron Age in date, but it cannot possibly be any later (**46**).

Herd instinct and the fear of Dog

Certain truths are self-evident. One of these is that sheep and other farm livestock become more docile and easier to manage when they are closely confined in a group. That is why farmers push and squeeze as many animals as they can into a truck or trailer. Despite the views of vociferous and uninformed critics, it is far more cruel to treat farm animals, take sheep for example, as woolly-coated humans; it is doing them no favours to give them the solitude and space *we* would normally require. When we first had a ram of our own, for exmple, we used to keep him in a paddock on his own. He hated this and would pace up and down the fence, in evident distress. It took us a day or two to work out why he was so upset, but eventually we understood. So after a few days we gave him half a dozen castrated (wether) lambs as companions, and he calmed down at once. The point to note is that sheep and cattle are herd animals — remove the herd and you remove their protection, or, more important, their sense of security.

Once they have been confined in a small space it then becomes possible to work with animals and to sort them into the various categories that you, the farmer, require. Now

46   *Close to the wetland edge and at the very end of the Fengate Main Drove we came across an area that had plainly been disturbed by the trampling of many animals' hooves, most probably in the Bronze or Iron Age.*

47   *A group of mouflon* (Ovis musimon)*, the near-wild ancestor of the modern sheep, in a tight group with the ram (large horns) adopting a protective stance.*

each species of animal requires it own types of handling or management setup. Pigs are often best handled individually, using a board to direct the head in the direction required. In the yard, cattle require very stout gates and railed enclosures, but they can be worked using pesistent dogs which bark and nip at their back legs. Corgis and bearded collies are traditional cattle-working dogs. I know enough about goats to know that they require very different handling in large numbers to sheep. They also consume everything in sight, including string, handkerchiefs and gloves. But that's all I know.

Sheep are well-known for being worked with dogs in the open, but it is less generally known that dogs are very useful in the farmyard too. Daily during winter I use my dog to remove animals from an area where I want to replace food; when the fly season starts I use her to move stock towards the dip bath which is concealed behind a special hurdle with a canvas flap 'door' built into it. The sheep know perfectly well that the dip is there, as they remember it from the previous summer, and they don't like at all. On my own, I would be hard-pressed to persuade unwilling ewes to take their annual bath, but my border collie, Jess, has powers of persuasion in her raptor-like eyes that I simply do not possess. I will say no more.

I have read it many times in the literature on ancient farming that primitive sheep cannot be worked with a dog. I have kept and still keep a few primitive sheep, including the near-wild ancestor of modern sheep, the mouflon (**47, 48**), and I have always been able to 'work' them all with a dog, both in the yard and in the open field, it seems to make no

48   *The reason for the tight group of mouflon and the ram's protective stance, revealed: Jess, my border collie, is giving them 'the eye'.*

difference (**49**). So far as I can make out, it is very basic to wild or feral sheep for the flock to gather together tightly when threatened from outside. Contented domestic sheep that have never known danger lose this instinct and scatter in all directions when danger, in the form of a dog, threatens. So they have to be re-introduced to it — a process known as 'dogging'. 'Dogging' is best done with a strong forceful dog, with sheep confined in a small area — perhaps a barn or a yard. I 'dogged' my sheep successfully in a paddock and it took a couple of days to train about 60. Once done, it never needs to be repeated and new members of the flock rapidly learn how to behave. Contrary to popular belief, sheep are far from stupid; in fact much of their so-called 'stupid' — seemingly irrational — behaviour may closely be linked to their strong herding instinct.

The process of dogging essentially consists of putting the fear of Dog into the animals, so that they clump together as soon as It enters the field. Lambs, are hopeless: they don't understand the rules; they rush around in all directions. They panic wildly and rarely form-up into clumps. In short, they are a dog-handler's nightmare. Dogs don't like them much either, and it has taken me a couple of years to teach Jess not to bite them — at least not too deeply or too often.

Before I bought my dog I went on a sheepdog handling course and there I learned that, when Jess or any other sheepdog rounds up sheep, what she is doing is entirely natural. When wolves gather at their lair the junior members of the pack will drive animals up to the Top Wolf who will kill them, take a bite or two and then throw the carcass 'to the

49   Jess rounds up a small group of mouflon sheep.

wolves', as it were. So in her dog's mind, Jess is fetching me my own sheep, to kill. What she thinks of me then, when I then refuse to bite into a hundred fleecy throats, is anyone's guess.

Collies have been bred to accentuate this gathering-up or herding behaviour, but the point I want to make is that it's not anything new or unusual. It's not a trick invented by some cunning medieval monk or circus animal trainer. Prehistoric farmers could perfectly well have observed the same behaviour in their own dogs themselves. In fact I'm convinced that's precisely what they did.

Managing and manipulating livestock

Most of the traditional ways of managing farm animals make use of their instinctive behaviour. As a consequence certain principles seem to apply, no matter what the age or period might be. Evidence for droving, batching, confining, inspection and sorting is plentiful in the layout of most British prehistoric field systems and it says much about the scale, state and organisation of pre-Roman livestock farming. I have touched on droving and confinement, and I shall discuss batching, inspection and sorting shortly. But there is one other thing to mention before we return to the archaeological evidence. By and large if an animal doesn't want to do something it won't do it, unless you can trick or fool it in some way. It sounds devious, and it is; but generally it works. Neolithic and Bronze Age farmers knew this too.

Before I return to the nitty-gritty of prehistoric livestock farming, what may we infer about ancient attitudes to animals? There is, I think, little doubt that the eating of meat was a high-status activity, but what about the animal behind the meat, what about ordinary, day-to-day attitudes? Were they cruel, off-hand, kind — how did they react to livestock? Obviously it's very hard to reconstruct such things from archaeological data, but I remember being struck by the discovery of the body of a young woman, aged 20-23 in one of the ditches associated with the Main Drove system (**50**).

Her body lay on the very bottom of the ditch, in precisely the same way as a cattle skeleton that we found in one of the droveway ditches south of the Main Drove (**51**). Had the cattle bones been treated with the same reverence as the young woman? We can never know, but it is interesting, nonetheless. For what it is worth, I have a gut feeling that the Bronze Age farmers of the Fens, knew their job well and did it very to a high standard. I find it hard to reconcile such a practical, efficient (in modern terms) approach to farming with wholesale, or recurrent cruelty, malnourishment or abuse.

The season of 1973 was very important to the development of my understanding of the Fengate pattern of livestock farming, so I will treat it in some detail. Early in the campaign we found a seemingly incomprehensible mini-droveway which ran down part of one edge of a Bronze Age field (**col. pl. 5-7**). I will refer to this mini-drove as a 'race', for reasons I will explain shortly.

It consisted of two closely parallel and very shallow ditches, about 1.5m apart and 25m long. At first, and indeed second, glance it seemed to make no sense whatsoever: it led nowhere and came from nowhere. So I wrote it up in the *Second Fengate Report* and forgot about it. Then, over twenty years later the truth dawned on me — largely as a result of my own farming experience in the intervening period (**52**).

Even in 1973 I had realised that the fields in question — they were known as the Storey's Bar Way system — had been laid out and used to handle livestock. For a start, every field was entered by a corner entranceway (**col. pl. 8**), and even with my limited experience of helping around the farms of my various relations, when a child, I knew that it was very difficult to persuade animals to leave a paddock, if the gate was set at or near the centre of a field's side. They would simply 'miss' the gate or bunch and spread on either side of it; getting lambs through such a gate (and I have just one on my farm) is almost impossible and the process drives the sheep, and the poor dog too, to distraction. A corner entranceway uses the sides of the field to form a natural funnel and animals pass through it rapidly and with a minimum of hassle. I know of no particular advantage in having a corner entranceway to an arable field.

Now there were certain things about the Fengate 'race' that made me think it served a special function, that had nothing to do with getting animals to move from point A to point B. For a start, it was neatly recessed into the side of the field in a thoroughly purposeful way which would not have interfered with the day-to-day use of the field. Its northern end was stepped back from a pronounced kink in the field side and its southern end was aligned absolutely centrally on another ditch of the field's boundary. The arrangement of ditches at the southern end of the droveway looked to be deliberate and again purposful (**53**), but at the time when I excavated it, I couldn't think why.

Then a couple of winters ago I was sitting by a roaring fire at home, idly thumbing through a catalogue of farming equipment which had just arrived. I didn't need to buy anything myself, having spent rather too much money the previous winter buying a

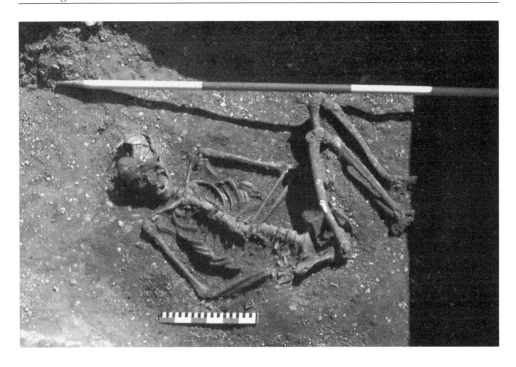

50   *The skeleton of a young woman, aged 20-23, found lying on the bottom of a Bronze Age ditch associated with the Fengate Main Drove.*

51   *Cattle skeleton found lying on the bottom of a Bronze Age ditch of the southerly ditch system at Fengate.*

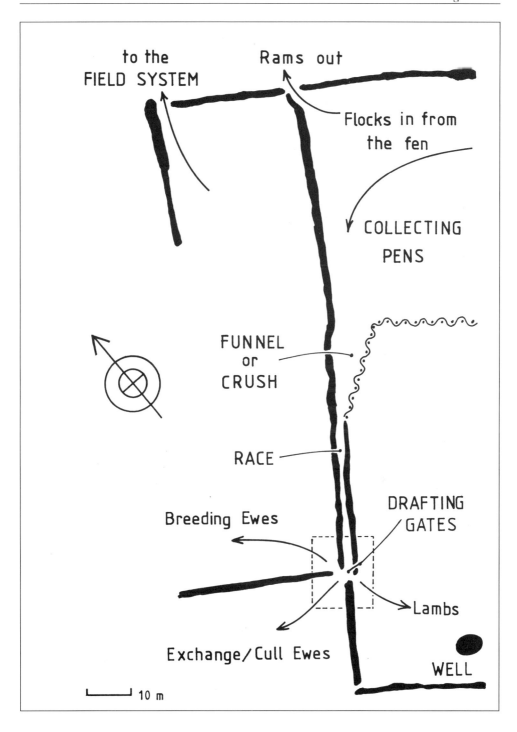

52   An interpretive plan of Early Bronze Age fields excavated at Fengate in 1973.

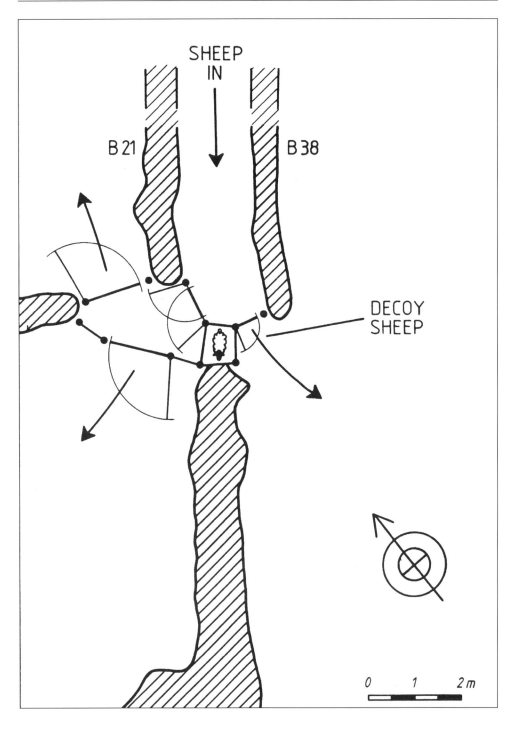

53   *An early phase of development of the Fengate Early Bronze Age 'race', showing how the three-way drafting 'gate' might have been arranged (ditches have been shaded).*

handling system designed to process about 250 sheep. So I leafed through to the pages listing the handling systems just to see whether the price of my equipment had gone up or down, when my eye fell on my *Second Fengate Report* which happened to be lying open on the coffee table. It was open at the page which showed the 'race'.

Then of course it jumped out at me, and I could have yelled Eureka!: the 'mini-droveway' of my report was a Bronze Age handling system. There could be no doubt about it. Suddenly the strange alignment of the droveway on the southern ditch became clear, as did the purposeful arrangement of features at the southern end of the drove. This was a three-way gate, known as a drafting gate today, whose purpose was to sort animals into different categories. Mine had cost me £200. I suspect the Bronze Age one was much cheaper.

The way the system worked was simple. Animals were driven into the narrow droveway from the north and there was probably a funnel-like arrangement of hurdles to help them squash in better. This funnel would today be termed a 'crush'. Animals would leave the crush nose-to-tail and would then pass into and along the narrow droveway, or 'race'. In the 'race' the animals could be inspected, they could be aged by looking at their teeth and their general condition could be assessed by feeling the muscles on their backs.

I would imagine there were perhaps a dozen or so people standing on either side of the 'race' examining the animals passing along it. At the far end, the three-way 'drafting gate' would probably have been fashioned by using children with hurdles; before I bought my own purpose-built gate, I would improvise with hurdles, pallets and visiting friends. I found that children were better with hurdles than adults because they were nimble and less easily distracted.

The important point to note about the 'race' we excavated in 1973 is that the whole thing was positioned in such a way as to give access to *three* fields or paddocks — not always a straightforward matter. Finally, although there is no direct archaeological evidence for it, there is space for a small hurdled pen within which would be placed a solitary (and usually rather fed-up) decoy sheep to encourage animals to pass along the 'race'. We still use a decoy sheep to entice in-lamb ewes to enter the scanning pen when our sheep are scanned to see whether they are to have singles, twins or triplet lambs. I would imagine a Bronze Age shepherd would readily have spotted the decoy ewe, but what he, or she, would have made of the ultrasound technology is anyone's guess.

Estimating populations

As a rule of thumb one can confine, for handling purposes, approximately two modern sheep to a square metre without causing the animals distress; maybe the figure for the much smaller primitive breeds would be twice that. This gives us a very rough guide for estimating flock sizes, *provided* (and this is very important) that one can reliably identify stockyards and handling systems on the ground, or from the air.

The main components of the stockman's handling equipment are scaled according to flock or herd sizes. A longer 'race' for example will handle larger numbers of sheep more efficiently. The one on my farm is intended to handle 250 sheep and is seven metres long. Very large flocks are best handled in batches. I recently met a shepherd from New Zealand

and she and a shepherd assistant handled her flock of 5,000 sheep in batches of 700-750 at a time. So one must try to look for evidence of batch handling, such as a large yard where the animals are loosely confined, a smaller yard or yards where they are more closely confined and a handling system area where they are very closely confined.

Finally, in situations where pasture was managed by restricting animals within fields or paddocks, it is possible to come to very approximate estimates of population, simply by estimating the numbers of animals it would have taken to keep the grass 'eaten down' and in good, short condition, but not over-grazed — in other words minimum and maximum populations. On established lowland grassland, using no artificial fertilizers, it would be unwise to keep more than seven breeding (primitive) sheep, plus their lambs, to the acre (17 ewes per hectare). Even in prehistory, when primitive sheep were less than half the size of their modern counterparts, I suspect such high stocking levels would have been unheard-of. As I said in the Introduction, on my own farm I run about four modern ewes to the acre and this is regarded by older farmers in the area as being quite intensive.

So to what extent *can* one use the features of the ancient stock farmer's landscape to estimate the size of past flocks or herds? When I first came up with the idea I was wildly enthusiastic and reckoned that it ought to be possible to be very precise. But that was in the initial flush of enthusiasm, and under such circumstances optimism can be tolerated. Almost two years have passed since I published the bare bones of the concept in the journal *Antiquity*, and now I would be rather less sanguine. I think the approach is very useful for determining the general scale or character of past livestock farms: in other words are we talking about subsistence farming with tiny family flocks, or larger scale mixed livestock/arable farming, or extensive ranch-style husbandry or something more akin to intensive livestock farming? Put another way, the approach could help to determine whether past flocks or herds may be numbered in tens, hundreds, thousands or even tens of thousands. But I wouldn't attempt to go any further.

Anyhow, using this approach I came to the conclusion that the Fengate field system was laid out to manage and graze thousands, not hundreds of sheep. The actual numbers would depend on a large number of factors, such as the extent and condition of the nearby summer pasture in Flag Fen, but hazarding a guess, I would estimate that the local livestock population was most probably considerably less than 10,000 animals — even at the height of summer when all lambs were present. So if we assume a conservative maximum population of around 5,000 ewes and lambs we may also assume that each ewe had on average a single lamb each year. I would therefore estimate that the breeding population of sheep in and around the archaeologically-visible parts of the Flag Fen basin in the Bronze Age was in the order of 2,000-3,000 beasts. If we allow for the large, archaeologically invisible areas of land swamped by the City of Peterborough the original, prehistoric figure could be double or triple that number. I think this gives an impression of the order of magnitude of the livestock population.

We will see later that this rough estimate of livestock population can be matched in other parts of the region. The implications are, however, considerable. We are not talking about subsistence farming, in which a few dozen or so animals were kept, together with some cereal crops. No, the evidence suggests fairly intensive livestock farming which was probably similar in scale to what happened in medieval times when wool from sheep grazed in Fenland pastures caused people from far and wide to call Peterborough Guildenburgh, or City of Gold.

Livestock populations and wealth

Now it could be argued that the large sheep population merely meant that the animals were kept for their numbers alone, and that their physical condition or fitness was irrelevant. I do not believe for one minute that this was in fact the case, but I shall return to the topic in a later chapter because I do think it merits closer attention. So, if we assume for the time being that the animals were kept in good condition and that the meat, wool and milk they produced were in demand, then it stands to reason that local communities must have been reasonably prosperous. Certainly the lengths people went to in order to parcel up the landscape were extraordinary and if the richness and diversity of the many objects thrown into the waters of Flag Fen are anything to go by, then a proportion at least of the community were well off.

So what was the underlying source of this prosperity? In medieval times it was a combination of factors, which included the right breeds of sheep, an appropriately organised countryside and above all, strong links with the craftsmen in the Low Countries who converted the wool to cloth. This was combined with what today we would call an excellently organised marketing structure here in England, based in Norwich and London. Clearly the picture was nothing like so complex in the Bronze Age, but equally clearly things had been 'got right'. Let me explain.

For a start, the breed of sheep was right. What precisely it was is still uncertain, but I would suggest it was an early improvement on the Soay — who knows, perhaps something more akin to the coloured Shetland? I have kept Shetlands for seven years and sometimes quite intensively. They behave well in large flocks, are very disease-resistant and lamb easily. Their meat is fine-grained and very tasty, and their wool also is fine and easy to spin. All in all they are a superb breed, and with more hardy Soay blood in them, I suspect they would have been more resistant to pneumonia than the pure Shetland.

The landscape was well organised for livestock farming and the people themselves had a social structure and dispersed pattern of settlement that complemented the animals' annual cycle. It was not until the heyday of intensive livestock farming had passed, during the onset of the Iron Age, that people began to live in nucleated settlements — villages — of any size. The Iron Age settlement pattern was much better suited to a style of mixed farming which had to provide security for easily stolen winter foodstuffs, such as grain. That is not to say, of course, that the new settlement pattern was necessary solely to protect winter food supplies, but it must have helped.

Perhaps the most important factor that contributed to the development of intensive livestock farming in the Fens and in other lowland areas, was the availability of seasonal grazing. In our area this was provided in large measure by the huge expanse of Fenland pastures; elsewhere it was the river floodplains, before they became too frequently inundated and choked with sticky alluvium. Sometime just before the onset of the Iron Age, the previously assured summer Fen pastures began to become less reliable. The summer seasons of rich grazing became progressively shorter, as water levels rose all over

Fenland. But while it lasted, from say 1800 to 600 BC at the fen margins, and somewhat later on higher ground, the regime of wetland/dryland seasonal movements allowed large numbers of animals to be kept — and to be kept well.

Livestock populations and prestige

In the previous section I came to the conclusion that animals were farmed for what they could produce and not as part of some glorified head-count, where numbers alone mattered. But there is a corollary to this. If animals were kept, for example, for their meat, did that confer some kind of prestige on the person who owned or controlled them? This is a very difficult question to answer, but there are some indications to suggest that the eating of meat was considered a high status activity in the later Bronze and Early Iron Ages, so presumably the people who produced or controlled the supply of meat were potentially in a very powerful position.

There is now much evidence that feasting was becoming increasingly popular during the Bronze Age and that the feasts were accompanied by the deposition or 'sacrificing' of fine metalwork. Some of the finer metal objects directly reflect the important role that meat played in such feasts. At Flag Fen one such object was a fleshhook, somewhat resembling a fisherman's gaff (**col. pl. 9**). These are rare items, but one found in the southern Fens — also probably a votive offering in water — was found close to a large bronze cauldron.

Cauldrons were a particularly elaborate and high status artefact at this time and must surely be closely linked to feasting. I would estimate that some of the larger cauldrons would easily accommodate the jointed meat of one and possibly of two Soay-type primitive sheep — with room for barley and vegetables! Dr Stuart Needham of the British Museum (who excavated the extraordinary, and very high status, riverside Bronze Age site at Runnymede Bridge, near Egham in Surrey) is of the opinion that the meat consumed there was more probably beef than lamb or mutton. This would tend to confirm that it was meat-eating that mattered, rather than the consumption of any particular type or species of meat.

8 Down in the Deepings

Into Lincolnshire

We have already visited the Welland valley a few miles north of Peterborough, where we encountered the Neolithic landscapes of Etton and Maxey. We will now cross the river into Lincolnshire (**54**), where we will discover that the landscape is exactly the same, to wit: a flat river floodplain with low-lying 'islands' and a sinuous fen margin. We have two sites we must visit: West Deeping and Welland Bank, near Deeping St James. Incidentally, the word Deeping comes from the Early English word for 'deep or low place'.

Both these sites are still being written-up, so I must be careful not to jump to hasty conclusions. Having said that, I think it is fairly clear what was happening at each. But first I should say a brief word about my own role in both projects.

Although I was very interested and made regular visits, I did not take an active part in the West Deeping project, other than to offer advice when the Director, Dr Jonathan Hunn asked for it. I suppose you could describe my involvement as at arm's length. I have, however, been very closely involved with Welland Bank ever since Tom Lane, head of the Trust for Lincolnshire Archaeology's contracting section, asked me whether I'd be interested in being the project's Consultant Director.

At the time Tom posed the question I was in the process of stepping back from running the tourism side of Flag Fen which was beginning to dominate my life. I was getting desperate to return to field archaeology and Tom's offer could not have come at a better time. 'Consultant Director' sounds very smart, but essentially it meant that I kept an eye on the archaeological strategy of the dig. To do this I would visit the site three afternoons a week. When the dig finished, in November 1997, I then had the responsibility of producing the final report which I'm currently busy with. Happily, I have a superb team to work with, and I'm enjoying myself immensely. It's certainly a huge improvement on tourism.

West Deeping

West Deeping lies on the edge of the Welland floodplain, about $9\frac{1}{2}$ miles (15km) north-east of Fengate and about 5 miles (8km) upstream (due west) of Deeping Bank (**55**). When I was doing my initial research before the Maxey and Etton excavations of the late 1970s, I had a good look at the air photos of the West Deeping site, as it lay just a mile north of where I was about to dig. To be absolutely honest, I think I would much rather have dug

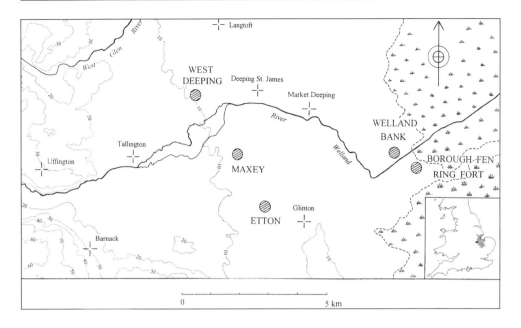

54   Map of the lower Welland valley showing the main sites discussed.

West Deeping: the cropmarks showed an extraordinary range of field boundary ditches, whereas Maxey seemed to be composed largely of Bronze Age ring-ditches and barrows (the Etton causewayed enclosure had yet to be discovered). Then, as now, I was more interested in where people lived and farmed, than where they laid their dead to rest.

Jonathan Hunn has been kind enough to let me have computer-rectified maps of the air photo cropmarks (**56**). The excavations showed this field system to have been in use in the later Bronze Age and Early Iron Age, but the actual starting date is still unclear. There are several probable Bronze Age barrows and ring-ditches spaced at regular intervals throughout the field system, as at Fengate, and I would imagine that the fields probably came into existence sometime after, say, 1500 BC. At this time the barrows would have been important features of the landscape.

The ditched and hedges fields are themselves *most* remarkable. They cover no less than 630 acres (255ha) of the modern arable landscape. If the air photos had been taken over Fengate, large areas would have been obscured by factories, housing and old gravel workings; but at West Deeping there is nothing modern (unless one counts a Roman villa and other archaeological bits and pieces) to distract the eye. The map is dominated by five — perhaps six — narrow, double-ditched droveways that run more-or-less north-south, at right-angles to the river floodplain, just as at Fengate. Towards the south-east the large-scale or open plan of the fields gives way to a system of smaller paddocks, divided into two, possibly three, groups by two droveways (which are less distinct than the main ones to the north-west).

A consistent feature of all five or six parallel droveways is the presence on each one's western side of a farmyard, which can be shown in at least three cases to have been sub-

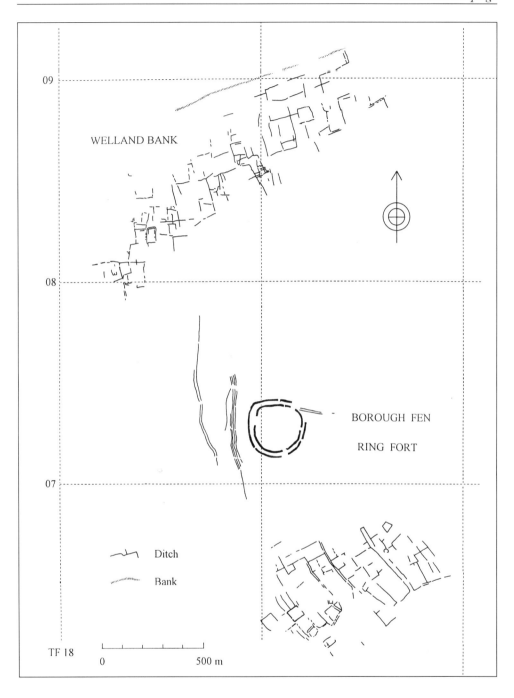

09

WELLAND BANK

08

BOROUGH FEN

RING FORT

07

Ditch

Bank

TF 18

0   500 m

55   *A map of cropmarks on the Crowland peninsula. Note the large Iron Age 'ringfort' at Borough*
      Fen (map by courtesy of APS).

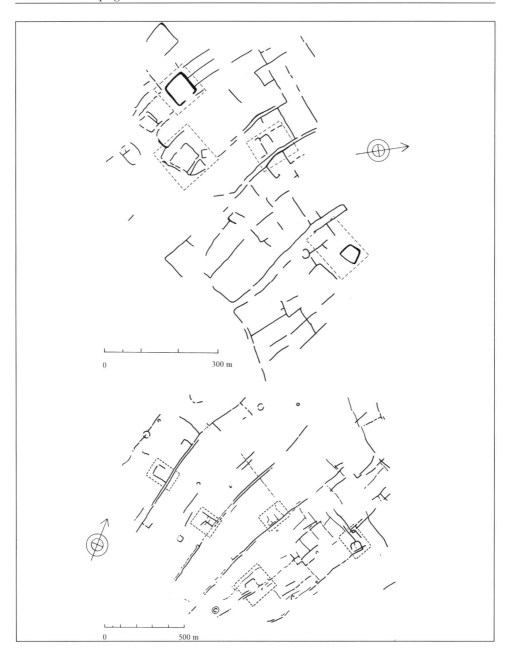

56   *Two examples of closely similar Bronze Age fields, plotted from marks in growing crops, taken from air photos. The lower plan shows the field system at West Deeping in the Welland valley floodplain of south Lincolnshire. The landscape is parcelled-up by double ditches droveways and each drove is served by a farm stockyard (within dashed line frames). The precise course of the river is still uncertain, but it probably flowed NW-SE, in the lower left part of this plan. The upper plan is of fields in Borough Fen with possible farm stockyards (within dashed line frames).*

divided in a manner which suggests batch-handling, with yards of decreasing size. The fact that each farmyard is on the same side of an individual drove, and that none appear to share droves, suggests that the droveway 'belonged' to the farmyard. Certainly there is no evidence for the wide, communal, droveways that one finds on old maps of the medieval Fens.

As yet we do not have details of individual livestock handling systems to work with, so we can only attempt to draw conclusions from the air photo evidence, but as at Fengate I think we are talking about thousands of animals — and perhaps a rather greater population than at Fengate. West Deeping is one of the most remarkable areas of ancient grassland farming in Britain. The organisation of the landscape is extremely tight and great efforts have been made to keep individual flocks and herds apart. If the area of floodplain available for summer pasture was smaller than, say, Flag Fen and Fengate (as would appear probable), then the high degree of organisation on the flood-free winter pastures might reflect a concern both to conserve grazing and to keep animals moving around within each farmer's land. It is a highly organised system of land partition that would make most medieval farmers jealous. I would dearly love to farm it myself.

If the population of beasts was as high as it would appear, then intestinal worms would soon have become a problem and this might help to explain why animals were moved around within each farmer's holding. Essentially the build-up of intestinal parasites can be slowed down considerably if land is allowed to lie fallow for at least three weeks, thereby breaking the life cycle of most worms. It does, however, takes a very much longer period of fallow to eradicate worms altogether. I suspect that, like most farmers today, Bronze Age farmers learned to live with them. The name of the game is, and was, containment.

The later Bronze Age sees a sudden expansion in the amount of salt being processed at sites along the Lincolnshire coast. Most of this salt was doubtless for human consumption or for preserving meat, but it is just possible that some was given to animals in the form of licks. We know that some salt was put into pottery containers which would have been ideal for use in a field — the high potash lick I give my ewes to aid conception at tupping time comes in plastic tubs which I position around the fields. 'Grassland staggers', a condition found when sheep eat lush grass in wet periods (it mainly strikes at springtime), is a mineral deficiency which can be avoided by the judicious use of licks.

The West Deeping field system went out of use in the Iron Age, but precisely when in the Iron Age is not altogether clear at this stage; the landscape is notably higher, in terms of metres above sea level, than either Fengate or Welland Bank and the effects of rising groundwater levels in the Iron Age may not have been felt either so severely or as early, as in lower-lying areas.

Welland Bank

The site at Welland Bank lies in a gravel quarry, some 5 miles (8km) downstream from West Deeping (**54**). West Deeping was at about 7-8m above sea level. Welland Bank on the other hand sits at a mere 2-3m above sea level. Unlike West Deeping the prehistoric land surface at Welland Bank lies deeply buried beneath about half-a-metre of clay alluvium.

Welland Bank is positioned on the landward side of a low-lying 'peninsula', which

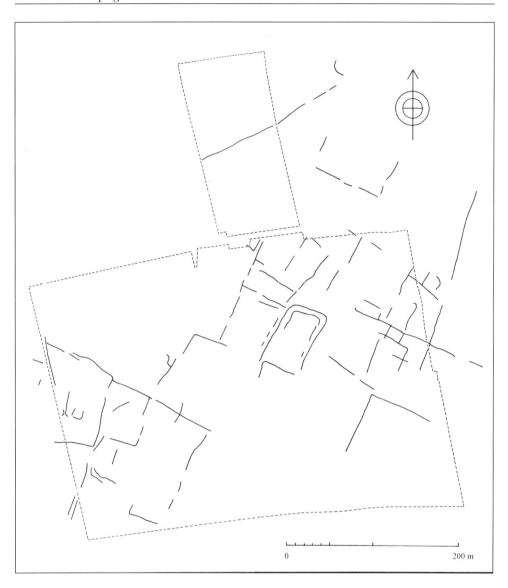

57   *Welland Bank Quarry: the cropmarks on the air photos were very slight. These few lines represent the remains of a major Bronze Age settlement and field system. Compare this plan with what was found in the excavations (58).*

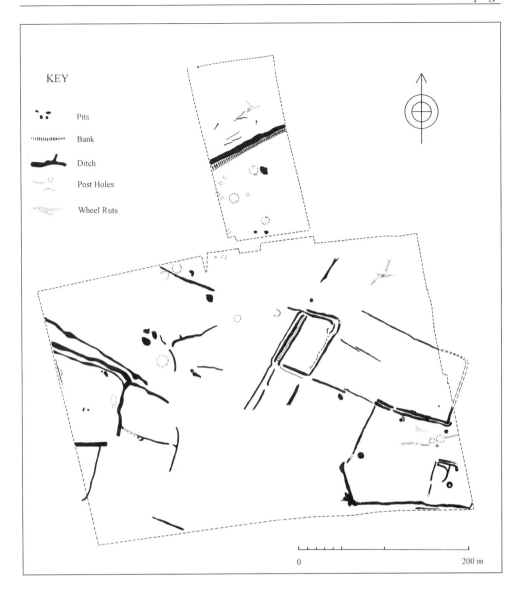

KEY

Pits

Bank

Ditch

Post Holes

Wheel Ruts

0   200 m

58   *Welland Bank Quarry: general plan of the main archaeological features revealed in the excavations*

includes the medieval abbey of Crowland B (**55**). Today Crowland is a small and very charming market town whose character has not yet been destroyed by suburban supermarket development. The straight, artificial course of the modern river Welland flows between the town of Crowland and the site, which gets its name from the huge river banks which skirt the quarry, on its southern side.

The quarry operators, Ennemix Construction Materials Ltd., were very generous indeed towards the archaeological team and much of the credit for the project's success must go to them. As a result of this close collaboration we now have an extraordinarily detailed picture of farming life in the Bronze Age.

Before I discuss our discoveries at Welland Bank in greater detail I must place the site in its geographical context. As I said, it sits on the landward or western side of the Crowland 'peninsula'. It was an area of some importance in the Bronze Age. To the south are the Bronze Age field systems of Borough Fen that closely resemble those of Fengate, and quite probably may even have formed part of the same system. Long, narrow droveways are an important feature of this landscape (**56**). A particular point of interest is the way that at least two of the droveways open out when they reach the edge of the wet ground, precisely like the Main Drove at Fengate.

The site itself sits within a somewhat dissimilar field system which covers almost two square kilometers. The fields here have fewer droveways and the ditches tend to be large — massive even, but the air photos are hard to interpret accurately because of the deep alluvium which tends to blot-out detail (**57**). Just how much detail was blotted-out was revealed when we completed the excavation and were able to draw up a detailed plan of our results (**58**).The difference was remarkable. On the whole I would guess that the fields and stockyards were primarily intended for the use of cattle, or sheep and cattle, but not sheep alone.

The remarkable archaeology of Welland Bank may best be approached by way of an extraordinary discovery made at Flag Fen, which incidentally is just visible on a clear day from the top of the Welland bank. It can be dated to around 1300 BC, and is possibly the earliest wheel known from Britain (**col. pl. 10**). Its diameter was 900mm (approximately 3ft) and its construction was very sophisticated indeed, but the details of its design are by no means unusual elsewhere in Europe at this time.

The body of the wheel was made from three planks of alder; the two dovetail braces that tied the three planks together were in oak and the locating dowels that kept the main planks in place were in ash. Each wood type was chosen for its particular characteristics: alder for its ability to withstand abrasion and rot, oak for strength and ash for flexibility and strength. The year before we discovered the wheel we also found part of an oak axle and the wooden lynch pin which prevented the wheel from coming off the axle.

The wheel and axle together suggested to Maisie Taylor, our woodwork consultant, that the vehicle concerned was small, perhaps the equivalent of a light cart or trap, but only big enough to carry a single person. However we didn't know certain basic things — whether, for example, the vehicle was two- or four-wheeled.

In the summer of 1996 the Welland Bank excavations revealed very shallow parallel grooves filled with pale grey silt , directly below the alluvium (**col. pl. 11, 12**). At the time it was thought they may have been wheel-ruts, but opinion was divided. Then in 1997 we

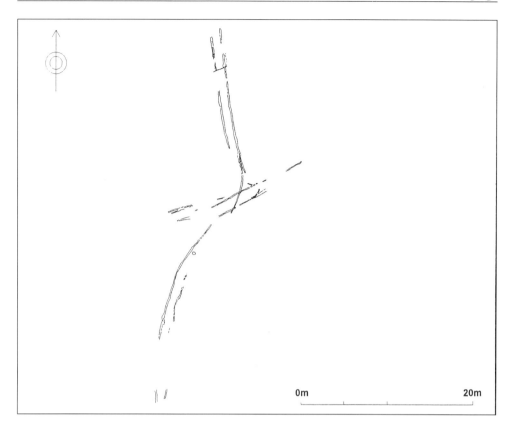

0m   20m

59   *A plan of the later Bronze Age wheel-ruts at Welland Bank Quarry. The ruts were made by*
      *a small, two-wheeled vehicle whose axle width was 1.10m (*plan by courtesy of APS*).*

found more of the strange marks and this time there could be no doubt whatsoever (**59**). The ruts were clearly made by a two-wheeled vehicle and the 'gauge' (or distance between the wheels) was 1.10m — just as it had been in the previous season.

The wheel-ruts really are most remarkable. Indeed anything so slight and ephemeral from so long ago is always extraordinary. We cannot be certain about their precise date, but we can say that they must pre-date the laying down of the alluvium, which probably happened in later Iron Age times. My own view, based on their relationship to known features of the Bronze Age landscape is that they belong firmly within the late Bronze Age — perhaps somewhere in the two centuries 600-800 BC.

The wheel ruts were found within a field system which vaguely resembled those at West Deeping and Fengate (insofar that it was a system intended for the containment of animals), but the size of the ditches and the general scale of the landscape indicates that the fields were originally intended to deal with cattle rather than sheep. Air photos show that the Welland Bank Bronze Age field system covered several square kilometers. It went out of use sometime in the Early Iron Age (perhaps around 500-600 BC?) when conditions became too wet for permanent, on-the-spot farming. As we have seen, there arc always archaeological problems when it comes to establishing a field system's starting date, but at Welland Bank we are lucky because a major division in the landscape, that between wet and dry, was marked-out by a large earthwork which we have been fortunate enough to date.

The earthwork, because of its size, showed-up quite clearly on air photos. When we removed the overlying alluvium (**col. pl. 13, 14**) we found that it consisted of a deep ditch (**col. pl. 15**), the bottom of which was still partially waterlogged. Gravel dug from out of the ditch had been thrown to one side where it formed a substantial bank. When viewed from above, the earthwork could clearly be seen to follow a gently sinuous course and it is possible that it was actually following the bed of an old stream. The dating evidence suggests that this earthwork was dug in the Early Bronze Age, perhaps around 1500 BC. The Early Bronze Age was a period when water levels in the Fens were beginning to rise, and we can see the earthwork as a physical boundary between the wet land to the north and the dry to the south. Maybe the bank served as a high and dry perimeter road that could if necessary be patrolled.

We removed the alluvium using large machines in the spring of 1997 and revealed directly beneath it an extraordinary dark deposit full of charcoal, pottery and animal bone. Rather unimaginatively we christened this deposit 'dark earth' — because that is what it was! The 'dark earth' covered an area of about three acres (**col. pl. 16**). It seems to have been very evenly spread, and our soil scientist, Dr Charles French, reckons the dark material — probably hearth sweeping, household rubbish and manure — was deliberately added to the soil to make it lighter and easier to cultivate. If he is right (which I'm sure he is), then the extent of the 'dark earth' may mark the actual area of cultivated land that belonged to this particular community. It was tiny when compared with the fields and paddocks laid out for and used by livestock, which covered square kilometers. Perhaps one ought to think more of cereal horticulture than agriculture *sensu stricto*.

'Dark earth' is rapidly becoming a major research interest in archaeology. It comes in two forms, an old-established urban 'dark earth' and, of recent years, a rural 'dark earth'. The rural species seems to occur most frequently in the Late Bronze Age and is found in the Fen basin and also in Wessex. Is it all the same stuff? Frankly we don't yet know, but Welland Bank should help us find out. For comparative purposes we know of another 'dark earth' site next door to Welland Bank. It is known as the Borough Fen ring-fort; both the fort and the 'dark earth' it encloses are of Middle Iron Age date (say 350 BC). I would not be surpised to learn that the fort has roots going back to the Late Bronze Age, but this is something I will have to demonstrate. The Borough Fen ring-fort is an extraordinary site, with a massive (and sometimes double) ditch and bank, which form a rough circle when seen from the air.

There is nothing like the Borough Fen ring-fort for miles around — in fact it closely resembles an upland hillfort, in all but location (at 2m above sea level it must be the lowest hillfort in Britain!). Presumably it was the home-base or capital of a local tribal chieftain and its position was carefully selected in order to cut-off the Crowland 'peninsula'. Anyone passing that way could not fail but be impressed by this extraordinary site rising up in the midst of the fens. In 1982 Charles French and I cleaned the grass and vegetation from a dykeside that cut through the ring-fort, and there we revealed a foot-thick

(300mm) layer of 'dark earth', sealed below a layer of alluvium (**col. pl. 17**).

When we cleared the grass off the dykeside, the half of the ring-fort where we worked was not protected by Law, but now I am delighted to report that the entire fort is a Scheduled Ancient Monument. It must be one of the best-preserved Iron Age sites in northern Europe.

We did everything we knew to the Welland Bank 'dark earth': we fingertip searched it (**col. pl. 18**); we took phosphate samples, we did a highly detailed geophysical survey, we sieved it and we took hundreds of botanical and other samples. Eventually, when we could do no more we removed it. Below the 'dark earth' we found one of the best-preserved Bronze Age farming settlements in Britain [60].

Now the way in which people arranged their settlement at Welland Bank seems to have been very different from Fengate, which is just 6 miles (9.5km) to the south. Instead of single, isolated farmsteads dotted throughout the fields, at Welland Bank we had a large settlement consisting of perhaps a dozen houses, some of which were rectangular and would have housed both people and livestock (whereas roundhouses accommodated people or livestock alone). I now believe that the different pattern of settlement reflects the fact that the Fengate houses were three or four centuries earlier than the Welland Bank village. Very recent work in Fengate by a team from Cambridge University has revealed a similar Later Bronze Age village which would appear to be precisely contemporary with Welland Bank. But what does this switch from isolated to grouped settlement mean, and why did it happen? More to the point, does it matter?

The answer to the last question is a resounding 'Yes'. The switch from isolated farms to small villages is termed 'nucleation' and it would seem to have happened in our area around and about 700 or 800 BC. It was an important change in the way people organised their settlements which may in part have been caused by increasing wetness on the land, but it may also reflect a broader, pan-European, social change in which a growing elite of powerful individuals were able to exercise political control. Essentially they wanted the members of their clan, tribe or chiefdom — all of which may have been growing quite rapidly at this period — to reside close to them, for reasons of control and influence, as much as defence. A castle in the middle of nowhere says little about the person living there, but place it on a hill dominating a client village and see how the tithes and tributes pour in!

From a farming perspective the switch from isolated farmsteads dotted around the fields, to villages with cereal gardens, suggests a gradual change from pretty well 'pure' livestock farming towards a type of farming, which although not 'mixed' did at least have a significant non-livestock element. Perhaps this part of the changing lifestyle may have owed a great deal to the gradually increasing wetness under foot — certainly by the onset of the Iron Age, when Welland Bank would have been under water for several months each year, the pattern of farming was very much closer to what we today would regard as 'mixed' farming, which is approximately 50:50 arable and grass.

The farming settlement below the 'dark earth' at Welland Bank consisted of round and rectangular houses, but there were also a number of deep, bowl-like sunken hearths which produced enormous quantities of charcoal, which in turn gave the blackness to the 'dark earth'. At the time of writing we are still not absolutely sure about these bowl hearths and

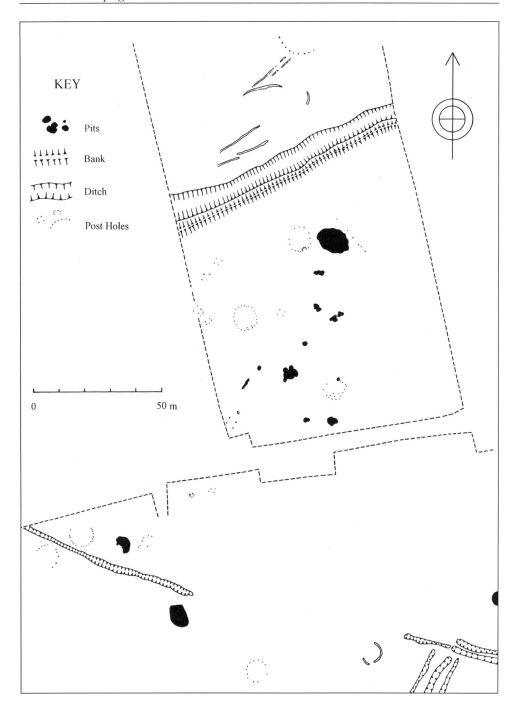

KEY

Pits

Bank

Ditch

Post Holes

0   50 m

60   *A plan of the Late Bronze Age 'village' settlement at Welland Bank Quarry (plan by courtesy of APS).*

what their precise purpose was. They *may* have performed some industrial function, but we can definitely rule-out their use in metal-working. We know they were not used for boiling-up salt water for salt, nor for smoking meat. So at present we are at a loss. The trouble is, we have little comparative material to go by, as very few later Bronze Age settlements have been found buried intact below alluvium. My own feeling, shared, I think by many in the team, is that the ash and hearths were part of the ordinary domestic scene — it's just that this type of evidence very rarely manages to be preserved.

One of the more remarkable features of the Welland Bank landscape was a rectangular double-ditched enclosure which showed-up clearly on air photos. It measured very approximately 75m by 45m and it appeared to have been carefully positioned with regard to the surrounding fields and paddocks (**61**). Results from an early exploratory trench led us to believe that it was three or four centuries later than the Bronze Age fields, but when we came to excavate it properly we had to discard this theory — it was clearly part of the same system and was in use at precisely the same time.

Normally speaking, one would expect such a carefully laid-out and substantial a feature in the landscape to have been part of a human settlement — perhaps an enclosure around an important person's house — or a small defended hamlet. In the event, we found no evidence for domestic occupation whatsoever. The main area of 'dark earth', about 80m north of the enclosure, had revealed about nine thousand finds, yet the enclosure ditches surrounding the site produced about enough pottery to cover the palm of a child's hand. And they were deep ditches, too (**col. pl. 19**). I was amazed: normally I'd expect to fill several boxes of pottery and bone from features as large as this.

The enclosure was entered at the corners and this is what held the clues to its use: it was undoubtedly intended to be the main stockyard for the 'dark earth' settlement and we even found the foundations of a small Bronze Age roundhouse just outside it. Maybe this little house was where the herdsmen lived who kept an eye on the animals in the enclosure.

I can well understand why such an enclosure would be positioned down-wind of the main settlement area and why such care should have been taken to confine the livestock, as wandering animals would rapidly cause havoc among the 'dark earth' cereal plots. Perhaps, more to the point, the enclosure would have deterred rustlers. In some pastoral societies rustling is almost an approved activity. It takes place in the autumn, when animals are most plentiful and it offers young men a chance to excel in the martial arts. I can well imagine that it must have been excellent sport — and a splendid way to impress young women.

As I have said, I presently think that the Welland Bank landscape was laid out to manage cattle, although animal bones found on site show that sheep and pig were also present in some quantity. The rectangular enclosure would have been large enough to hold the community's animals — perhaps 100-200 head, or something of that sort. But it is interesting that there is no evidence at Welland Bank for individual farm stockyards, as one finds at Fengate, and most particularly at West Deeping. This might suggest that cattle farming was organised on a rather different, perhaps more communal basis, than sheep. It might also tell us something about the way the management or tenurial arrangements of individual farms altered, following the move from dispersed to nucleated settlement.

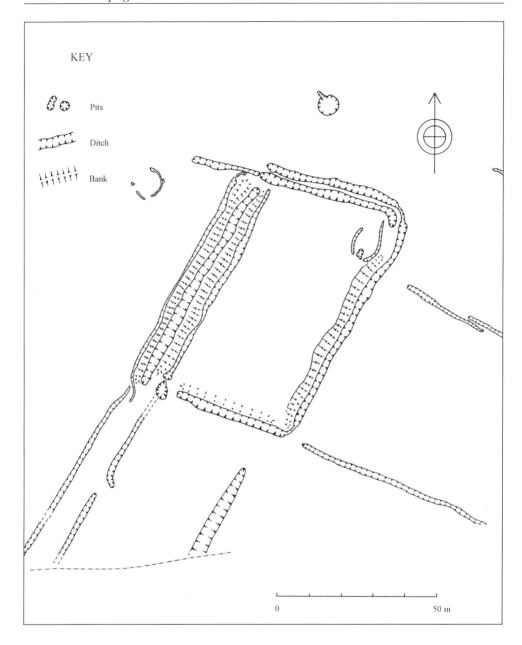

KEY

        Pits

        Ditch

        Bank

0   50 m

61   *A plan of the Late Bronze Age rectangular enclosure at Welland Bank. Before excavation we thought it would prove to be a defended settlement, but on investigation we found no evidence at all for domestic activity and we are now forced to the conclusion that it was constructed for the management and protection of the livestock that belonged to the nearby Late Bronze Age 'village' (*plan by courtesy of APS*).*

Maybe it would have been simpler to manage cattle communally than sheep? I don't know at this stage. At all events, I think that the social and organisational changes involved in the switch from dispersed to nucleated settlement at the end of the Bronze Age would have affected rural communities just as much as the upheavals of the Enclosure Movement three millennia later.

We still await more precise dating, but it would appear that the Welland Bank ditched fields and paddocks were abandoned by the start of the full Iron Age — perhaps by 500 BC — and we can be reasonably sure that the main local cause of this was increased flooding. During the last five centuries before Christ, the wide floodplain of the braided rivers that together comprised the Welland system would have flooded regularly. During these wet times the available grazing of the floodplain meadows would have contracted to the higher fringes towards the edge of the valley. Under such circumstances a modern farmer would be advised by his bank manager to diversify — which is precisely what happened to farms in the area, in the latter part of the first millennium BC.

9 On markets, marriage and memorials

Markets and exchange

By the later Bronze Age (the centuries around 1000 BC) we are in a landscape that would have been familiar to us today: there were small hedged fields, droves and trackways, even roads. True, houses would have been made from wattle-and-daub and farm animals would have been very much smaller than the huge beasts that graze the fields of late twentieth-century England, but the bare bones of the lowland landscape would be familiar — we would not be walking through open clearings within a dense mantle of forest.

We must return to the Flag Fen basin after our brief excursion into Lincolnshire. But we must also return to a theme that was raised when we discussed the layout of the very much earlier causewayed enclosure at Etton. To recap briefly, the causewayed enclosure was divided down the centre into two halves, east and west, and I suggested that the western half was used for public events and the eastern for private or family rites. In some instances the two halves may have been used separately, but in most cases I would suggest that the public and private gatherings took place at one and the same time.

We have seen that in the world of farming markets are public gatherings, but they are also events where people renew old personal friendships. Similarly the great feasts of the Christian calendar such as Christmas are times when people come together, but they are also occasions when we commemorate those near to us who have recently departed from this life. More secular modern occasions, such as Armistice Day, witness society paying its respects to the Unknown Soldier and to the military dead in general, but a rapid glance at the damp eyes in a Poppy Day service congregation soon shows that many men and women have their minds on more personal memories. Put another way, public assemblies and private or family gatherings often go hand-in-hand, and I believe this basic human tradition has a very long history indeed. Let us now think about the archaeological implications of this.

The phosphate survey of the main ditched droveway at Fengate showed it to have been a muddy 'piss-mire'. When Dr Paul Craddock told me about it all those years ago, I was interested, of course, but I failed to grasp the true archaeological importance of what he was telling me. Such a trampled, grassless surface can only be produced by large numbers of animals using the droveway for several days in succession. A small number of animals, using the drove regularly, would have worn sinuous narrow paths, but they would not have reduced the droveway surface to a 'piss-mire'. By the same token, a large flock driven along the drove once or twice would not have reduced it to such a state.

Turf is, on the whole, remarkably tough and resilient — as any cricketer will tell you. No, to wreck the grass surface of the droveway would require large numbers of animals using it for more extended periods; maybe even for days at a time. They may even have been housed or penned upon it — and this, I think, provides a clue on how the Main Drove could have been used.

I now believe that the Main Drove, the subsidiary droves that ran parallel to it, and the double-ditched paddocks or small enclosures that formed the rest of the system, may together have comprised the Bronze Age equivalent of a livestock market. I think its location, *across* a major boundary drove, was also significant. This was more than a private, or farm, stockyard which would have been placed within its own 'territory', as on the air photos at West Deeping. It was placed across a major boundary and it thereby transcended the local land divisions. That fact alone places it in an entirely different category.

Of course in Bronze Age times there was no such thing as a modern market economy. For a start, there was no money to buy things with. But it went further than that: the idea of bidding against other buyers in an open auction, would have been very foreign. From what we know about pre-market economies it would appear most probable that the exchange of livestock would have been governed by other, largely social, factors.

The main social consideration would have been the reinforcing of inter-family ties that had been brought about through marriage. In other words livestock, in the form perhaps of 'bridewealth', would have accompanied people as they moved from one family to another. It would also be a mistake to assume that 'bridewealth' payments were necessarily one-off transactions; in many tribal societies people 'paid for' their wives or husbands on the instalment plan. The whole purpose of these transactions was to hold society together, so it made sense to extend the process as much as possible — even in some instances beyond the grave.

Exchange or mart

If the transfer of animals from one community to another did indeed take place mainly to cement various social alliances, then it would also have been very important to ensure that as many people as possible witnessed the transaction. There is little point in completing something as significant as a social transaction without the actual moment of exchange being witnessed and acknowledged by everyone. As we have seen before, prestige and status would also have played a part in the process, just as they do today. An example should make the point.

At many modern markets, the auctioneers or breed societies organise fatstock competitions. Fatstock are lambs or steers in the peak of condition and ready for slaughter. Usually the animals entered in the competition come from among the pens being offered for sale. A special area of the market is set aside and everyone present on the day — buyers, sellers, market staff and visitors — will make a point of paying the competition pens a visit. Once judging has been completed, the names and addresses of the winners and runners-up are displayed at the appropriate pens, together with a rosette, certificate, trophy cup —

or whatever. To win such a competition is important, and success carries much weight with the people who matter – and, to most farmers, the folk who matter are the butchers and meat company buyers.

Winning fatstock contests is important, but so also is the prestige of buying the animals in the winning pen; I always enjoy visiting the self-proclaimed Best Butcher in Town after the East of England Show. There I will see the First Prize carcasses proudly displayed in his shop, complete with rosettes and certificates. And of course the price the butcher paid would have been *way* above what the meat itself was worth. But he would not have been buying just meat when he paid out that money — and everyone who witnessed him pay on the day of the show knew that and applauded him loudly when the bidding ceased. As I said before, it's all about prestige and status.

In the Bronze Age, the criteria for selecting good animals would probably have been different. Today we judge beasts by the quality of their presentation, and most important of all by the set of their musculature, which is generally known as their 'conformation'. In sheep, for example, the meat lamb buyer would be looking for broad, rather square hindquarters with a good thick upper part to the back legs. In the remote past we can only guess at what constituted a 'good' animal, but I would guess that the animal's general sturdiness, health and vigour would always have been important; nobody would ever have accepted a sick or lame beast; indeed, to pass on or exchange such a beast would probably have been considered an insult.

It is however possible that the appearance of individual animals counted for little, and that numbers, or flock/herd size alone, was all that mattered. In certain parts of Africa, for example, a man's social standing is largely determined by the *number* of beasts in his cattle herds — the larger the herd, the bigger the man. In these societies it is unheard-of actually to slaughter animals. This approach to animal husbandry tends to encourage over-grazing — which is damaging of itself — and it can result in numerous under-nourished, skinny and disease-ridden animals. It is entirely possible that such under-nourishment would leave distinct clues on the bones that survive in the archaeological record, but to my knowledge there is as yet no clear evidence for it from sites in Britain.

Having said that, nobody has systematically looked at large numbers of archaeological bones with this sort of problem in mind. It has to be a high priority for research, but it will not be simple to achieve. Certain basic questions need first to be asked: what, for instance, are the osteological clues — for example, marks on the bones — that would indicate slight, moderate or severe under-nourishment and physical stress? Anyhow, insofar as we can tell at this stage, there is no strong evidence to suggest that prehistoric livestock were grossly under-nourished. This would indicate that they were kept for what they could provide their owners, namely, meat, wool, hides, blood, bone and antler. The first three are self-explanatory; the latter three require brief explanation.

Blood is a naturally rich source of converted energy, iron, vitamins and minerals. Certain cattle-herding societies, such as the Masai of Kenya, routinely bleed their livestock using specially designed chisel-shaped arrows that leave a shallow, clean wound. It should be remembered that primitive cattle did not have as long a lactation as modern cows and it is quite possible that there were social taboos against removing a calf from its mother's milk early — if at all. Under these circumstances blood could have provided an important

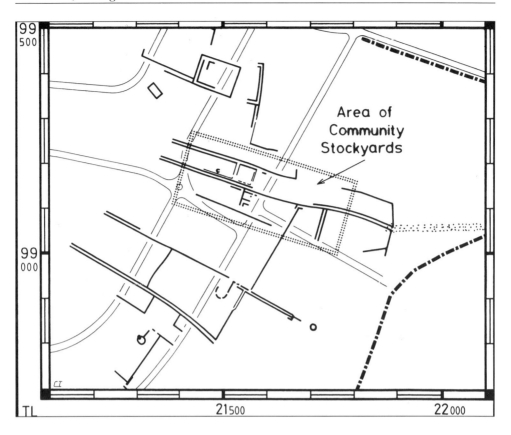

Area of
Community
Stockyards

62   At the centre of the Bronze Age field system at Fengate was a complex of intricately arranged droveways and enclosures that are thought to have formed a 'market place' or series of community stockyards on either side of the Main Drove. It has been possible to excavate about one third of the community stockyard system (63). The position of the Flag Fen post alignment is shown to the right of the Main Drove.

— and renewable — foodstuff.

Today we live in a world where many small portable objects are made of plastic, but in the past bone and antler would have been used instead, for example, for handles and hafts, and for pins, needles and spoons. With time and use bone tends to become brittle, but antler is an extraordinarily dense and durable material, and is known to have been prized in antiquity. Perhaps it's also worth mentioning here that animals other than cows alone would have been milked; sheep, in particular, produce a very palatable, rich and sustaining milk.

So, to sum up, in prehistoric times, livestock 'markets' would have been places where farmers, their families and friends met at regular intervals to exchange animals and to indulge in a little inter-family and person-to-person rivalry. The business of livestock exchange was deeply rooted within the structure of society and would, I am convinced, have mirrored the jockeying for position and power within society in general. For this

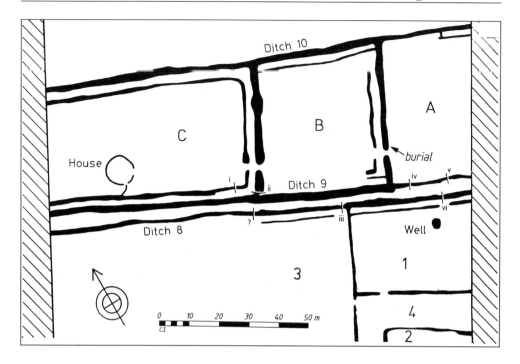

63   *A plan of the excavated portion of the Fengate Bronze Age community stockyards. The lower case Roman numerals indicate the position of possible blocked gates or entranceways.*

reason I have called the Fengate Bronze Age livestock market a series of *community stockyards* (**62, 63**). They were places where farmers from all over the local community and beyond could meet to exchange livestock, and negotiate other social deals, such as marriages, which would, in their turn, lead to further movements of livestock. Thus the wheel of rural life rolled on, relentlessly.

Flag Fen and the farming landscape

The extraordinary site at Flag Fen has been mentioned several times and I will now attempt a brief description of what it was, and how it fitted into the farming world. I am often asked the simple question 'What was Flag Fen?' and people are invariably disappointed when I say that a simple explanation is impossible. They assume that the reply is a cop-out, but it isn't. If I were to reply that Flag Fen was a Bronze Age equivalent of a Fenland hillfort — for it has many points in common with such sites — they would depart happy. But what if I were to shout after them, 'What were hillforts?' Then they too would be forced to prevaricate. The point is, the term 'hillfort' is a description, it is not an explanation, and poor old Flag Fen doesn't even possess a description. So to return to the question, Flag Fen was all sorts of things to all sorts of people, but of one thing I am quite sure: nobody would have taken it for granted.

The medieval and modern city of Peterborough has grown-up at the point where the river Nene flows off the clay and limestone uplands of Northamptonshire and enters the flat, peaty Fens of Cambridgeshire. The transition from dryland to wetland was very gradual and this, as we have seen, was where Bronze Age farmers constructed their elaborate field systems. Just east of the Fengate 'shore' was a large natural island formed of stiff blue Oxford Clay. Today this island is the location of the modern market town of Whittlesey, together with the numerous clay pits of the local brick industry.

The low-lying land between Whittlesey 'island' (for it is now all drained and dry) and the Fengate 'shoreline', formed a low-lying and shallow basin which was named Flag Fen after the wet-loving flag irises which once grew in abundance there.

Now, to cut a long story short, my team and I were working our way along a drainage dyke in the middle of Flag Fen in November 1982. We were carrying out a survey for English Heritage in which we examined freshly cut dykesides after the Drainage Board had dredged them out with mechanical excavators. As we walked carefully along a dyke we came across several large timbers protruding from the side, about a metre and a half below the surface. At the time we were approximately half-a-mile (1km) east of the Fengate 'shore'. It then took us several years' work to realise the size and significance of our discovery, as the entire site was so deeply hidden from view by layers of peat and alluvial silts.

We have since been able to date the timbers very precisely, using dendrochronology, or tree-ring dating, and we know that they were driven into the muds of Flag Fen during the years 1300-900 BC. In other words it would appear that the site was maintained in use (and so far as we know continuously) for some four centuries.

I shall summarise what we currently think is the 'true' picture, but Flag Fen has a habit of proving our explanatory hypotheses wrong — so treat what follows with caution. I suspect it will take several more decades of research to crack the many mysteries presented by this extraordinary site.

The Bronze Age timbers which we came across in 1982 can now be seen to have formed part of a thick, wall-like barrier of large posts (**col. pl. 20**) which crossed Flag Fen from the 'shore' at Fengate to a promontory of Whittlesey 'island', known as Northey. The distance between Fengate and Northey is just over half-a-mile (1km) and so far as we know most of the posts survive below the surface intact. Unfortunately their survival is now under threat because of land drainage.

The post alignment traversed a narrow strait of wetland which in effect formed the principal entrance to the main Flag Fen basin from open fens to the east. The Flag Fen basin itself would have been the prehistoric equivalent of common grazing in medieval and modern times. When the Nene flooded in winter, the pastures of Flag Fen would be naturally enriched by a thin layer of fertile silt. At this time of year the flocks and herds would be driven to the slightly higher ground around the edge of the basin, where the large numbers of animals would be carefully controlled within the ditched and hedged fields. As soon as warmer weather came and the waters retreated, animals would be driven back out into the Fen to fatten. In medieval times, as in the Bronze Age, it was absolutely essential that the farmers who lived on the edge of the basin had full control of their summer pastures. Without the two parts of the grazing cycle working efficiently together, the whole system would soon collapse.

10 A bridge across the Styx

The Flag Fen post alignment

The wall-like barrier of posts at Flag Fen has been described as a post 'alignment' — a term that was chosen because it carries less meaning than 'wall', 'barrier' or 'roadway' — all of which are things the structure might simultaneously have been. The post alignment is about 10m wide and is composed of five roughly parallel rows of posts. Each row seems to have been rather different: the central row was so densely packed with posts that it probably did indeed form a wall. Posts comprising the rows on either edge of the alignment were inter-woven with wattle and may well have formed a strengthening or reinforcing revetment. Another row was about 2m wide and it is thought that its posts could have formed an irregular palisade rather similar to the outward-leaning mass of sharpened posts that protected the English archers at Agincourt.

We started detailed excavation of the post alignment in 1984 and it soon became clear that it was an enormously complex site. At the point where the posts entered the water, the ground surface was built-up and consolidated by tree-trunks which were laid on the muds that formed the bed of the fen. The trunks were trimmed of branches and were held in position by stakes and smaller posts that were driven-in. Above this 'log layer' were several layers of roundwood which served to raise the surface perhaps six inches (say 15cm) above the water. On top of the roundwood were layers of planks (mostly oak), many of which had been dusted with sand and gravel, doubtless to prevent feet from slipping. Nothing can be more treacherous than slimy wood.

There were as many as three walkway surfaces of this sort and most ran close by the central wall-like row of posts. So it would seem that the post alignment was both a defensive barrier and a trackway, but in 1989 we started to make a number of extraordinary finds which could not possibly be explained-away as casual losses — as items that had dropped accidentally from travellers' bags or pockets.

The point where the post alignment meets the dry land at Fengate was particularly important. The posts hit dry land at the precise spot where the main droveway from the community stockyards opened-out at the edge of the wet land. It could not have been neater, and coincidence is impossible. Both post alignment and droveway were orientated in the same direction. There could be no doubt that the junction between the two had been planned deliberately.

Wealth in the waters

We used a local metal-detecting club to carry out the first detailed search amongst the timbers at Flag Fen and found some 320 metal objects, mostly Bronze Age and made, predictably perhaps, of bronze. They were not the sort of things that one might expect to have been 'lost'. Instead of small trinkets of little value (in other words, the Bronze Age equivalents of pen knives, key rings, nail files and cigarette lighters) we found swords, rapiers, daggers, jewellery, axe-heads, spearheads pieces of a metal shield and so forth (**col. pl. 21**). To make matters even more puzzling, nearly all these objects had been deliberately damaged before being dropped in the water.

We mapped the precise location of each object and it soon became clear that they were found either amongst the timbers of the post alignment, or else along its southern side. None were found north of the alignment — *ie* towards the open fen — the direction that any trouble might be expected to come from. This distribution was very odd. If the alignment had been a road, then one might have expected objects dropped by travellers along it, to have accumulated more or less evenly on both sides. So there was no getting away from the fact that the metalwork had been placed in the waters deliberately, most probably as votive offerings of some sort.

I suspect the bronzes were placed into the shallow waters not so much to placate hypothetical 'water deities', as to join the world of the ancestors. Water was the 'looking glass' through which objects, souls and even people passed in order to reach the Other Side, whence, of course, there was no return. So the objects that were offered-up were very special indeed and there is evidence that they were very carefully placed in the water. They certainly were not hurled, like the Sword Excalibur. Some of the items found at Flag Fen are most remarkable and bear testimony to the prosperity of Bronze Age farming communities in the area. A small gold ring — possibly from a composite earring — may well have been made in central Europe. There are also numerous small objects in tin, including three miniature spoked wheels which were most probably made in or around the Alps. Several other objects were almost certainly imports from continental Europe.

While the presence of imported objects bears testimony to the long-distance contacts of the farming communities who provided them, the sheer volume of metalwork and other valuable items is astounding. So far only a small proportion of Flag Fen has been thoroughly excavated — the proportion must depend on the true extent of the site which is still somewhat uncertain, but I would guess it's around 5-7% — and we have found about 320 bronzes. This would suggest that there are still perhaps 5,000 more waiting to be discovered.

This profusion of expensive metalwork throws new light on the relative prosperity of our livestock farmers. Of course they could have given *all* their most valuable possessions away to the ancestors, and have retained little or nothing for themselves; but even so — and I have to say I consider that hypothesis most unlikely — they were nonetheless able to generate very considerable wealth. And what is more, I do not believe that the inhabitants of the Flag Fen basin were necessarily unique. I am sure that other lowland farming communities in Britain would have been just as well off. Certainly, recently published sites in spots as far apart as Surrey, south Cambridgeshire and Oxfordshire

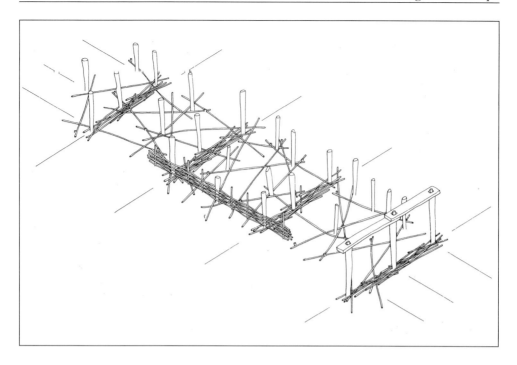

64   *A schematic drawing of an early phase of the Flag Fen post alignment showing the transverse partitioning into segments or 'rooms'. One partition was probably marked by a lintel or superstructure supported on three large alder uprights.*

suggest that many Bronze Age farmers were doing very nicely indeed.

'Rooms' out of doors

The great gardener Vita Sackville-West famously laid out her garden at Sissinghurst, Kent, in a series of small hedged 'rooms', each one of which had its own distinctive character. As the visitor perambulated the grounds, the 'rooms' would provide a series of sometimes quite surprising contrasts. In fact the notion of 'rooms' was so successful that it has become quite a cliché of modern garden design — so much so that I run a mile when I read that a new garden has been laid-out in this way.

About five years ago I was, as is my wont, trying to do too many things at once. During the day I worked in the garden of my newly built house, and in the cool of the evenings I tried to write the text of the definitive Flag Fen report for English Heritage. I don't know whether my dislike of garden 'rooms' had got the better of me, but one evening I noticed that the plans of the Flag Fen timbers I was poring over, showed distinct signs of partitioning into — yes — well defined 'rooms'. The five axial rows of posts went one way and a series of transverse horizontal timbers clearly went another. In other words, the transverse timbers and wattlework comprised partitions.

I was able to distinguish four possible partitions which were separated from each other

65   *An unused saddle quern from a group of four placed close to a partition wall beneath the Flag Fen post alignment. Note the stone-dressing marks on the face nearest the camera.*

by gaps or spaces of 5-6m length (**64**). The partitions sometimes formed small, low walls and were often marked by extra large posts. Perhaps most remarkably of all, they were further marked-out by carefully placed offerings such as a fine decorated sword scabbard plate or a group of four unused quernstones (**65**).

I think the post alignment at Flag Fen had two main roles. It was a barrier which prevented access into the common grazing that was reserved for the farmers living around its edge. It was also a dry route across a narrow part of the wetland. So why on earth partition it? Here I think the parallel of Sissinghurst-style garden 'rooms' works quite well. The purpose of the Sissinghurst 'rooms' was to draw the visitor along from one enclosed space to the next: so each 'room' had a clear entrance and exit. The Sissinghurst 'rooms' provided an intimate setting: the visitor was able to enjoy their charm and the many contrasts of colour, texture and scent, in peace. The 'rooms' were, in effect, enclosed, self-contained and private environments where people could linger for as long as they wanted.

The Flag Fen 'rooms' were also built to be private places, but I think their original purpose was rather more than mere pleasure.

The mystery of the Flag Fen platform

About 600m east of the Fengate 'shore' we found evidence for a large timber platform, over $2\frac{1}{2}$ acres (1ha) in extent, which was built at the same time as the post alignment which ran across it. I wish we understood the platform better, but sadly we don't. Much of what we do know is, however, negative. We know, for example, that it did not contain houses or dwellings and that it would not have been habitable during the wetter months of the year. It was by no means a continuous or solid raft of timbers and contained a number of ponds or wet spots — perhaps miniature, or 'tamed' wetlands where people could offer items to the waters, on their own terms, as it were.

But whatever its shape and purpose, the platform — and the post alignment passing through it — has so far provided us with the clearest evidence for partitioning. So what was going on out there, 600m from the Fengate 'shore' in one of the wettest, most low-lying parts of Flag Fen? I am convinced that the clue to the mystery lies locked within those partitioned 'rooms'.

We must imagine the Bronze Age visitor walking along the post alignment. He sets off from Fengate and after perhaps ten minutes of quite difficult walking he arrives at the platform and the entrance to the first 'room'. What does he see? I would suggest he finds himself about to enter a family shrine where offerings to the ancestors were made perhaps when someone died, or during the commemoration of an important family anniversary. It was a shrine destined for the use of the living, rather than a mausoleum where the bodies of the dead were housed.

At Etton special offerings — human skulls, models of skulls, complete pots, animal heads etc — were placed at the ends of the short ditch segments. The end of the ditch came to symbolise the limits or boundaries of the family; it was this boundary which gave the family its cohesion, its identity. For people living at the time it was the all-important difference between Them and Us.

At Flag Fen, amongst the partitions and the segments between them, we found many offerings which harked back to Etton: in particular there were whole querns and deliberately broken or complete pots which must surely be symbols of family life if ever such a thing existed? But there was also a new element which had appeared in the intervening two and a half thousand years, namely, the deliberate deposition of swords, spearheads and daggers. These are an entirely new lexicon of symbolic statements. They speak of a society where an *individual's* power and prestige was now of enormous importance. In pre-Roman times weapons were probably more to do with status and prestige, than something as ill-considered and wasteful, as fighting. They were more like the dress swords worn by officers in the British Army today: readily identifiable indications of rank and status.

Public and Private — apart

Now we have seen that the public and private worlds were celebrated at Etton on either side of the north-south central division. Private to the east, public to the west. But each half of the sacred area was enclosed within the single segmented enclosure ditch which ran around the outside. So we have an apparent paradox: public and private were separate, but they were also united together. At first glance the need to enclose might be seen as a defensive measure, but a ditch with gaps is not exactly an efficient fortification; instead, I see it as a way of isolating a very special place that was of great importance to the community. What went on there may also have been considered dangerous in some way; perhaps it was thought that certain groups — maybe children — would be at risk if they entered. So the site was deliberately placed in a remote part of the countryside, which was subject to regular flooding, and where nobody in their right mind would wish to farm or settle. But why was this? What activities could possibly be considered dangerous?

The answer lies, I think, in the private side of the enclosure. This was where we found abundant evidence for activities associated with death, and perhaps the afterlife too. If we are right in our interpretation that this was the place where souls started on their journey to the next world, the world of the ancestors, then it may well have been viewed by the community at large with dread. Even today, wartime concentration camps, execution chambers and so on are seen by even the most rational of people as aweful (using the word in its original sense). In such ghastly places one feels frightened and close to death; one is acutely aware of the transitory nature of life itself.

In many societies it is held that disease and other afflictions are punishments visited on the living by God and/or the ancestors, and that disease, or whatever the retribution might be, escapes from the next world when a new soul enters it. When a door is opened the traffic can be in both directions. Many societies believe that the retribution — whatever it might be — will arrive at the very spot where the recently departed soul made its last journey. Monuments such as Etton must therefore have inspired dread, but they were also perceived as places of actual danger. So they were located in hard-to-reach locations, on hilltops, near cliffs or deep within river floodplains — well out of harm's way and distant from settlements. I suspect that children and those who had not passed through the initiation rites into adult life would not have been admitted under any circumstances.

Both Etton and Flag Fen may be described as liminal. The Oxford Dictionary tells us that liminal means 'of or pertaining to a limen', which isn't very helpful. A limen is in effect a boundary; it is the threshold, for example, beyond which one can feel no pain. So the word can be used in two senses here. Both sites were liminal in their location — which was close to the edge of habitable farmland, in countryside where access could only have been seasonal. But they would also have been considered liminal in anthropological or theological terms — as places close to the edge of existence itself.

The public world of the seasonal livestock 'market' in the communal stockyards of Fengate was now placed where it belonged, on the dry flood-free land inhabited by ordinary farmers. There was now no need to remove it to a liminal place on the edge of the inhabitable world, as had been done at Etton. The private world, on the other hand, had become even more private and as ideologically liminal as it had ever been. Physically it was linked to the habitable landscape by the slenderest of ties and was placed well out in the deepest fen. This was where people retreated for their more intimate, family ceremonies, while the great public festivals took place around the community stockyards. I can well imagine how the silence of Flag Fen would have contrasted with the dust, hustle and bustle, crowds and flocks a few hundred metres to the west.

I would suppose it is entirely coincidental, but it is interesting nonetheless that the public area of Flag Fen, the Fengate community stockyards, was west of the private or family shrines out there on the platform, just as the public half of the Etton enclosure was west of the private half. People living at Fengate would have seen the sun rise across the waters of Flag Fen. It is hard to ignore the strength of such symbolism.

11 Further afield, in space and time

So far in this book I have tried to illustrate the complexities of earlier prehistoric farming, using examples that are intimately familiar to me. I would far rather write about what I have discovered myself, than what I have learnt from others, and I have never enjoyed reading second-hand research. But there is a danger that this approach can be too parochial. So in this chapter I want to examine the extent to which the type of intensive livestock farming discussed here was typical of lowland Britain as a whole. Then I want to move forward in time and briefly examine agricultural developments in the centuries following the Bronze Age.

Closer to home

The Wash Fenlands of East Anglia and south Lincolnshire were Britain's largest wetland, but they were once extraordinarily diverse. Today they give a very misleading impression of uniformity, especially to the outsider. The landscape is flat, mainly treeless and divided-up by countless deep drainage dykes. Recent research by the English Heritage Fenland Project has shown that the Fens consisted of a large number of micro-topographical regions, each one of which possessed its own distinctive style and character. In effect the Fens were divided into mini- and micro-fens.

The landscape comprising Fengate and Flag Fen is a good example of such a mini-fen. In its early stages it was kept wet by waters flowing into it from the river Nene which were lime-rich as a result of having passed through the limestone hills of Northamptonshire. Then, in Iron Age times and later, the region's natural seaward defences were broached by floodwaters that contained more than Nene water alone. By way of contrast, just 3 miles (5km) south of the Flag Fen basin, the mini-fen of Holme Fen had an entirely different type of history. Here the wetland was first fed by rainwater that drained off clay ground; this gave rise to a more acid-loving type of vegetation which would have provided far less nutritious grazing. This seems to have been the reason why there is very little evidence for Bronze Age farming round about. Eventually large parts of the area were inundated beneath the waters of Whittlesey Mere — England's largest body of freshwater until its drainage in 1850.

It would seem that each mini-fen had its own character and history, and there were probably dozens of them across Fenland, and each one different. At present we are at the very earliest stages of studying these mini-fens. We are still trying to gather the basic facts, just to define and characterise the problem. I think it will take a couple of decades to move on from this, to do the really interesting work, which will be about explaining why the mini-regions differ from each other and how they would have inter-related in antiquity.

So what is being revealed about farming elsewhere in the Fens? The first point to note is that the Fens are liberally scattered with finds of Bronze and Iron Age metalwork, just as at Flag Fen, and it is very tempting to suggest that much of this 'treasure' was deliberately placed there. Again, one does not need a degree in palaeo-economics to work out that the widespread deposition of such valuable items must surely indicate widespread prosperity. And the source of that prosperity? Surely, what else but farming?

Much of the evidence for ancient field systems comes from air photos and it is very often difficult to date cropmarks with any accuracy, so I will concentrate now on Fenland field systems, known from air photos, that have been reliably dated by excavation. A series of large-scale excavations carried out by teams from Cambridge University, under Chris Evans and others, has revealed evidence for large Bronze Age field systems in the floodplain of the river Ouse east of St Ives. The main site investigated to date is in a gravel quarry at Barleycroft Farm.

The work at St Ives is still actively in progress so it is difficult to be definitive, but the fields do seem to be rather different from those in the Fengate/Deeping Bank part of the world. Chris reckons that sheep were the main animal kept and that the fields were indeed laid-out for livestock, and date to the Bronze Age — but that is where the similarities end. There is less sub-division of the landscape, with far fewer droveways and the fields are far larger and evenly-sized; hedges seem to have been placed between small double ditches, in a strangely labour-intensive fashion. Having visited the sites in question, I agree with Chris' explanation — but I find it odd, nonetheless.

Then there are tantalising fragments, such as the ditched droveway and enclosures recently excavated at Block Fen, Mepal in the central Cambridgeshre Fens. Here the ditches contained washed-in silts and very little else, which suggested to the excavator that they had once been something to do with pastoral farming. A small, possibly Bronze Age barrow was shown to be later than the field ditches which would suggest that they could be very early indeed — maybe even Neolithic? That site urgently needs more research (I would love to get my hands on it).

Further afield

If the gravel terrace around the Fens and the floodplains of the rivers that drained into them were criss-crossed with Bronze Age fields — as seems to have been the case — then what about other lowland floodplains? Let us take as a case study the big one: the Thames. Of course London will have obscured things somewhat, but I'm glad to say, not entirely.

Like the Fens, the Thames has produced truly vast quantities of Bronze Age metalwork, much of which was dredged-up in the early decades of this century, when the river was deepened to allow ever-larger ships upstream to the Port of London. I think it is now generally agreed that most of this metalwork was placed in the river, or in the shallows near to it, during religious ceremonies similar in general principles to what was going on, at about the same time, in Flag Fen. Again the presence of metalwork in huge quantities surely indicates wealth. Now in the case of the Thames it is possible to argue that the wealth could have been generated from more than just farming alone.

By the Bronze Age, trade or exchange was of growing importance and the control of commodities, such as salt, must have been significant too. But having said that, recent research has shown that the Thames valley contained field systems as large in scale and potentially as complex as those in and around the Fens. Personally I am quite convinced that livestock farming was the basis upon which most of this astounding wealth was based. And perhaps I should justify the use of the word 'astounding'. The Thames on its own has produced more Bronze Age metalwork than many European countries — quite literally tens of thousands of objects. Had metal-detectors been available to the men working the dredgers, the mind boggles at what would have been found: as it is, only the larger, more unmissable items were recovered: spearheads, axes, swords, shields etc. At Flag Fen, where we were able to use metal detectors, the large items amounted to perhaps 10% of the entire assemblage.

When I was still a student I worked during one bitterly cold Christmas (1966, I think it was) at one of the most important sites in British archaeology. The site was in a gravel quarry near Grays in Essex and is known by its Anglo-Saxon name, Mucking. The name well describes conditions there that Christmas. To say it was cold would be to miss the point entirely: it was bone-chilling and unwarm-upable. That damp east wind, howling up the Thames estuary, hit the gravel terrace where the site sat, like microscopic bullets of ice. As I write, I can feel the chill cutting into my fingers. But it didn't seem to worry the site director Margaret Jones, nor the stalwart farmers of the Bronze Age, both of whom were made of sterner stuff than this student.

Mucking was *the* pioneer, large-scale, open-area rescue excavation. Margaret had no time for little 'keyhole' trenches. She worked on a grand scale, often with several acres stripped of topsoil. That way she could select what did or did not merit excavation. In amongst a wealth of Saxon, Roman, Iron Age and Bronze Age features were a series of quite small, and usually straight, field boundary ditches which could only be of Bronze Age date. Like Fengate, these ditches sometimes paired-up to form droves and often seemed to have been aligned on round barrows. When Margaret first showed me the plans I was immediately convinced that this was evidence for large-scale livestock farming, which was almost identical to what we were finding at Fengate.

Air photos of gravel sites elsewhere in Essex have provided contenders for other Bronze Age field systems, but to date these have not been satisfactorily dated through excavation.

London has of course obliterated the very slight evidence one would normally expect to find for Bronze Age fields. Having said that, the river through the city has produced masses of metalwork, while several Bronze Age barrows and even Middle Bronze Age cremation cemeteries are known from the suburbs. So people were living in the area, and presumably were farming there too. But if we are to find solid evidence for Bronze Age fields and farming then we would have to look west of London, beyond the urban sprawl.

I was talking about this book, and Bronze Age farming in general, to my old friend and colleague, Professor Richard Bradley of Reading University. In retrospect I must admit I was doing some gentle academic 'fishing', as I knew that Richard can be very generous with his information. Instead of the juicy nugget or two that I had expected, Richard positively enthused about the work of a graduate student of his, David Yates. So I wrote to him, and David generously sent me all manner of information which I will attempt to summarise.

David did his research by the direct route. He had read what I and others had done, and he wanted to learn if there were many similar Bronze Age field systems in the largest river gravel floodplain of them all. In 1980 a survey by Richard Bradley and John Barrett had shown there were just 9 sites with evidence for Bronze Age fields. So, armed with this survey, he visited all the archaeological teams who had been active in the world of commercial contract archaeology in the Thames valley. One major site (which I understand is archaeologically extremely similar to Fengate) could not be reported-on, for reasons of commercial confidentiality, but, that aside, David was able to reveal 34 new discoveries of Bronze Age fields or field systems. That makes a known total of 44 sites.

Now David Yates' work is important because it is structured research: he has been able to show that the sites form a pattern, or rather a series of patterns, and the patterns themselves make sense. In other words, he is not merely collecting new sites for their own sake, as others might collect stamps or credit cards.

The sites along the Thames valley west of London are contemporary with Mucking and with the Fenland fields further north. They come into existence by or during the Middle Bronze Age, flourish in the Late Bronze Age, but go into decline — perhaps quite rapidly — by the Bronze/Iron Age transition. I suspect that many might one day be shown to have origins that reach back into the Early Bronze Age, but it took us several years to prove that at Fengate, and the hectic world of pre-Planning excavation does not exactly encourage such introspective navel-gazing.

The sites fall neatly into four distinct and separate clusters, spread evenly — two and two — on either side of the Goring Gap, where the river passes through the escarpment of the Berkshire Downs and Chiltern Hills (**66**). The two groups downstream are named after well-known sites at Runnymede-Petters and Marshall's Hill; north and west of the Goring Gap are the groups at Wallingford and Lechlade. The occurrence of each of these four groups coincides neatly with concentrations of metalwork finds from the river. Each group would also appear to have had a higher status site as a regional centre. David has termed these 'Aggrandised enclosures' and 'Island settlements'.

It would appear that the apparent gaps between the groups are in fact real. A major excavation, for example, at Yarnton between the Lechlade and Wallingford groups revealed no evidence for formally laid-out fields. It would also appear that the groups were further distinguished by identifiable, individual styles of pottery. Each group must be seen as a self-contained livestock farming systems in which products were distributed internally and externally by way of the higher status 'market' centres.

Outside the four groups, the older and more extensive pattern of farming continued, much as before. But inside the groups David has been able to demonstrate a pattern of increasing complexity and intensity, again directly comparable with what we have observed in Fenland. But it would seem that the parallels can be even closer.

Landscapes compared

I first suggested the idea of community stockyards in a publication that appeared in June 1996. In that paper I was able to point to just two or three other sites in Fenland that might include something similar. David read the paper while working on his dissertation and

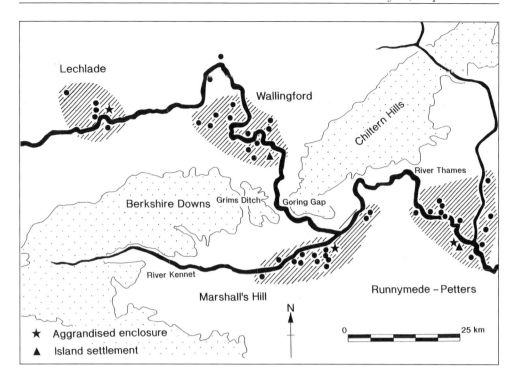

66   Map showing the distribution of Bronze Age field systems in the Thames valley upstream of London. The sites are found in four clusters (shaded) which coincide with concentrations of Bronze Age metalwork finds from the river.

was able to make a most persuasive case for community stockyards at four Thames valley sites: Dorchester on Thames, Field Farm, Moulsford and Lower Basildon.

At Fengate we found evidence for pre-Bronze Age aligned landscapes and perhaps these will be found in parts of the Thames valley. One thinks of the Dorchester area in particular, with its many Neolithic sites, but there must be many others, too. It will be interesting to note whether the hypothetical early landscapes follow the orientation of the Bronze Age landscapes — and if not, why not?

The new discoveries in the Thames valley are particularly important because they come from so huge an area. The disadvantage, of course, is that much of the evidence has already been destroyed by gravel digging and urban growth. Indeed, quite soon there will be little left to study. But how does the general organisation of livestock farming in Fenland compare with the Thames valley? First and foremost, in both areas the farming of livestock was intensive and highly organised; it was also economically successful. As David Yates has said, it was a society 'which may have used its agricultural surplus to support a programme of conspicuous consumption'.

The regional organisation of Fenland livestock farming is harder to discern, largely because we cannot be certain about the 'gaps' between known areas of ancient fields. In other words, were they real gaps, or merely areas where the evidence was hidden beneath accumulations of peat or alluvium? At present I can only clearly see two major groups: one in the southern Fens, around the Ouse valley, perhaps extending as far west as Mildenhall in Suffolk and another, from Peterborough in the south and then northwards along the edge of the Fens, into Lincolnshire for perhaps 25 miles (40km). Within these major groups there were doubtless smaller sub-groups, such as the later Bronze Age fields around the Lincolnshire Fen-edge villages Dowsby and Billingborough, midway between Bourne and Sleaford. Having said all that, I have the strong subjective impression that the organised farmed landscapes of the later Bronze Age Fens had begun to break free of the constraints imposed by the region's topography of mini-fens, small embayments and 'inlets'. In other words, from about 1200-1400 BC the field systems have started to reflect human geography and not natural topography alone. This is important because it shows that confidence was increasing and that farming communities possessed the practical knowledge to transcend many significant natural boundaries.

I have long been struck by the extraordinary similarities of the more intensive fields and handling systems of Bronze Age livestock farmers in lowland Britain, and I find it impossible not to believe that the farmers involved were not in regular and lose contact with each other. Maybe the networks were far wider than we presently suppose. Perhaps farmers in the Thames valley regularly exchanged stock with colleagues in the Fens?

I would imagine that the majority of stock movements were between farms within, say, a 10 mile (16km) radius, but sometimes new blood has to be brought in from right outside the area. This is particularly important in the case of bulls, boars or rams. As an old shepherd once said to me: 'look after your ram, he's half your flock'. We have no idea of the distances involved in such movements, but they could have been very considerable indeed — perhaps as much as a couple of hundred miles. It seems to me patently obvious that communities who were capable of arranging and constructing elaborate livestock farms and fields were also capable of organising an efficient road or droveway network between the various regions. Without good roads, it is difficult to see how such intensive farming systems could have operated effectively. For not only did they work well when they were set up, they then continued to work well — and for upwards of a millennium.

The problem of the Trent valley

I want now to turn to Britain's second largest lowland river valley, that of the Trent. By rights it ought to have been covered by a criss-cross of Bronze Age field boundaries, but to date none are known. It fulfills all the conditions: it's wide, flat, and the gravel soils are freely draining. It also has a broad floodplain and there are large expanses of alluvium. Normally these would have been ideal locations for the development of intensive livestock farms and field systems.

The area has always been archaeologically active, but recently the expansion of contract excavation has been extraordinary, especially at gravel quarries. Although large areas of the valley are covered by alluvium many have been investigated during commercial excavation and the results are always the same: there is no evidence for Bronze Age field systems. On the other hand, it is not as if the area was deserted in later prehistory.

The river itself has produced quantities of Bronze and Iron Age metalwork and there are at least two known riverside settlements of the period, either of which could turn out on closer investigation to have points in common with Flag Fen. A recent study of Bronze Age metalwork from the Trent near Nottingham, by Chris Scurfield, shows a distribution that strongly recalls the situation in the Thames west of London, with clear and distinct concentrations. There are also numerous Bronze Age barrows and barrow cemeteries. So what was going on?

We do know of several large field systems, but these all seem to date to the later Iron Age or Roman period. David Knight of the Trent and Peak Archaeological Trust tells me that they seem to have been fields for mixed farms, but ones where livestock was the most important component. Certainly the shape of the Iron Age Trent valley fields in no way resembles Fengate or the sites of the Fen margins, which, after all, are not very far away to the south-east. The Trent is certainly very much closer to the Fens than the Thames.

It could be argued that the absence is more apparent than real, that the fields were divided up by ditchless hedges which have left no archaeological trace. Given the level of archaeological activity in the area I find this hard to accept. Ditches do not have to be continuous to 'work', and several of the fields in the Ouse valley, for example, are bounded by intermittent or discontinuous ditches. But, having said that, I still find it hard to believe that no ditches at all were employed. But until we find some actual hard evidence to the contrary, I shall have to keep my belief to myself.

Taking the evidence as a whole I think we can safely suggest that the Trent valley was indeed farmed in the Bronze Age, but far less intensively than some of the other places we have discussed in this book. Boundaries were marked by barrows, and herdsmen would have ensured that the animals stayed within their owner's permitted pasture. Incidentally, I do not believe that this style of so-called 'open' pasture needs actually to have been open at all. At Fengate the pollen record shows that there were several episodes during the site's long history when grassland was replaced by open scrub, but not by woodland. This would suggest that the scrub itself provided a good environment for grazing, and of course the presence of animals in sufficient numbers prevented the regeneration of secondary woodland. Scrub can be a very important type of landscape and it is all too often ignored in the archaeological literature, where countryside is either 'open' or 'wooded'.

During the agricultural recession of the 1870s many fields in rural Britain reverted to scrub, but they provided nonetheless excellent grazing for livestock, and of course the various thorn bushes gave shade and shelter. Nowadays rabbits can destroy grassland in such surroundings, but this would not have been problem in the Bronze Age, as my least favourite rodents (give me a rat any day) were not successfully introduced to Britain until Norman times.

I would see the Trent valley as essentially similar to the gaps between the four main groups of Bronze Age fields in the Thames valley: grazed, but not intensively so and the countryside dominated by open scrub.

Miles away

The main purpose of this book, as I said at the outset, has been to discuss the origins and development of a uniquely British style of intensive livestock farming. That style of farming was confined, so far as we know, to lowland areas, but I do not want to give the impression that it was the only style of farming practised in Britain at the time. Indeed, far from it.

Remarkably intensive Bronze Age livestock field systems are known, for example, on the Yorkshire Wolds, Dartmoor and Salisbury Plain. Many of these quite closely resemble the landscapes discussed here: there are droveways, stockyards and other features of the pastoral landscape. The downland of Wessex, Sussex and Hampshire has revealed so-called 'Celtic' field systems which must surely have been used by livestock, to judge from the number of long, double-ditched droveways. The fields around the greatest hillfort of them all, Maiden Castle in Dorset, are a fine example of how to manage numbers of animals on thin chalkland soils.

In the more hilly or mountainous country the pattern of livestock farming was altogether different. Here, as today, the farms were smaller and the land was not able to sustain intensive livestock farming. Farmers worked to provide for themselves and their families. Their aim was to satisfy their own needs; they were not interested in earning a surplus. One example will illustrate the scale, but by no means the variety, of upland farming in the Bronze Age. It provides a striking contrast with the situation in the lowlands.

Working with his students from Cardiff University, Dr John Evans carried out a survey of archaeological features on the island of Skomer, off the south-west tip of Dyfed, in Wales. They were able to map the entire island and paid close attention to features of the farmed landscape and in particular to abandoned prehistoric farmhouses and farmyards. The countryside was peppered with small, discrete, stockyards, most of which were attached to farmhouses (**67**). The area of these stockyards was tiny by lowland standards and they could not possibly have held more than a few dozen sheep at any one time. The farming here is essentially independent and very small-scale; it is undoubtedly more to do with subsistence than surplus.

After the Bronze Age

Most prehistorians of early farming find it very difficult to use the conventional Three-Age system of Stone, Bronze and Iron, for the simple reason that the big changes in landscape development do not happen to coincide with the three major developments in technology. In particular the transition from stone-using (Neolithic) to metal-using (Bronze Age) technologies seems to have made very little impact on the practical business of farming the soil. So landscapes that were first broadly partitioned in the Neolithic were parcelled-up into fields in the earlier Bronze Age — but both were essentially part of the same process.

Some prehistorians believe they can see evidence for a 'new order' in society from Middle Bronze Age times onwards. Personally I can't. What I see is gradual change

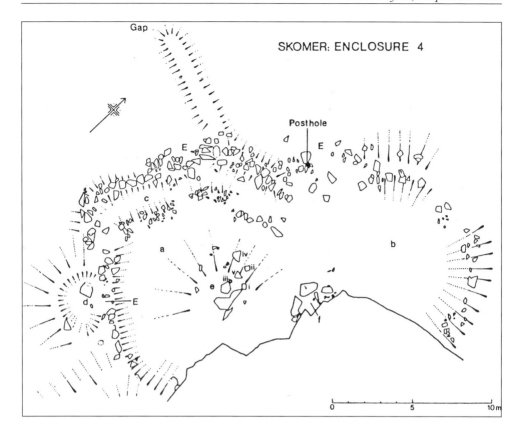

67   *A plan of a possible prehistoric sheep-handling yard on the island of Skomer, Dyfed* (after Evans, 1990).

through time. To be sure, during certain periods the pace hotted up and in others it slowed down, but essentially things remained much as before. I very much doubt whether there would have been perceptible change from one generation to another. Rural communities are conservative for a very good reason: it takes time to learn how to farm effectively and ill-considered, rapid change can often be disastrous. One experiments with caution if starvation is a possible outcome. Certainly I can see no evidence whatsoever for population change — invasion, migration, call it what you will — in the rural landscapes I have studied, between the Neolithic and Roman periods. Even in the Roman period, the rural Romano-British population remained strangely unaffected by the major political changes going on around them.

So far this book has mainly concerned itself with livestock, because I believe that it was by far and away the dominant form of farming in Britain between, say, 4500 and 600 BC. It seems to me that the evidence of field shapes and layout, of tracks and droveways, of stockyards and farmyards speaks eloquently of the prehistoric farmer's ability to control and manage animals. But there is good evidence that cereal crops — mainly wheat and barley — were also grown and processed. Having said that, however, I do not believe that the traveller through the Neolithic or Bronze Age countryside would have been greeted by many swaying acres of ripening corn.

The evidence for growing cereals derives mainly from the Middle and later Iron Age — after about 400 BC in very round figures. It consists of actual cereal grains from storage pits, or the by-products of threshing and winnowing which botanists have been able to extract from archaeological settlement deposits, such as floor sweepings etc. But the vast majority of such evidence comes from within settlements — or very close to them. This evidence tells us that cereals were eaten and were prepared. It does not tell us in what quantity this happened, nor indeed whether the cereals were grown *in situ*, where they were eaten — although it is usually assumed by most archaeologists that this was in fact the case.

The other main strand of evidence comes from pollen analysis. Again this tends to be a test of presence or absence. Cereals are grasses and in the past it was not always a straightforward matter to differentiate between the two; similarly pollen analysis has revealed the presence of many weeds of cultivation, such as the plantain, which are assumed to have colonised freshly disturbed ground — and by implication this is taken to mean ploughed ground. But it should not be forgotten that all farm animals, and not just pigs, can disturb ground very effectively too.

There are a few examples of plough-marks in the soil below barrows, the best known being South Street in Wiltshire. At Maxey we were able to show that the ground had been stripped of turf before a Neolithic oval barrow was constructed, and I am inclined to think that the plough scratches at sites such as South Street are so clear because they were freshly buried beneath the barrow. In other words, the criss-cross of plough marks was part of the ritualised preparation of the ground to receive the dead, in much the same way that turf was removed at Maxey. I would be far happier to argue for widespread arable in the chalklands if Neolithic and Bronze Age plough marks were regularly found beneath field boundary banks (lynchets) or other non-ritual elements of the landscape.

It is my belief that cereal cultivation did not become an important player in pre-Roman farming until well into the Iron Age. Why this was, is open to debate. It may have been a reflection on growing conditions, or on social attitudes to non-meat foods. It may have been something far simpler: the old system of livestock farming worked well and was suited to Britain's moist, Atlantic climate, so why change? The change when it came may in part have been a response to changing growing conditions and to improved varieties of cereal crops; but I have never thought these ideas were too convincing. A much stronger motivation was required to persuade farmers to abandon their old livestock fields and to lay out large areas of the countryside afresh. The main stimulus for change was, I think, population.

There is now abundant evidence that the population of Britain grew remarkably in the second half of the first millennium BC — from the beginning of Middle Iron Age times. The evidence is crude but unarguable: put simply it consists of a sudden increase in archaeological data (*ie* sites, artefacts etc.) belonging to the Middle and later Iron Age — of all sorts. There are settlements (hamlets and villages), farms, fields, fortified sites almost everywhere in the lowland zone.

This extraordinary growth of new information was apparent in the 1980s, but since the introduction of developer-funded projects late in 1989 it has grown so fast that nobody can stay abreast of it. It is generally supposed that, in order to support a rapidly growing later Iron Age population, it became necessary to diversify into mixed farming — a system much better able to support a larger population than animal husbandry on its own. In archaeological terms it would appear that the change towards mixed farming happened quite quickly and there is little doubt that it was in part a response to wetter ground conditions which would have affected floodplain grazing adversely. At Fengate the change happened in the course of perhaps two centuries, between about 1000 BC and 800 BC. It is of course entirely possible that the change of farming practices brought about the growth in population — and not *vice versa*. But one could argue that one until the cows come home.

The term 'mixed farming' is quite widely used today and it is often held up as an example of how farming ought to be done. It is seen as more ecologically friendly and less intensive. These attitudes spring largely, I suspect, from an idealised rural idyll that may never have existed. In my experience, mixed farmers have always done their very best to extract the most from both sides of their farms and have used the interplay of arable and livestock to wrest as much as they possibly could from the countryside. And good luck to them.

In the 'classic' British mixed farm, manure from the animals is spread on the arable fields; then cattle eat the longer grass and sheep follow, as they prefer closer grazing. But why should the mixing necessarily take place on or within *one* farm? Why can't I keep sheep and my neighbour grow wheat? He gives me flour and straw in exchange for manure, wool and meat. It's less self-sufficient — which Utopians might see as an ideal in its own right — but it does encourage communication and discourse between both individuals and communities. In prehistory I suspect there was far more mixing at this level: farmers in one area would tend to specialise in one thing — say cattle —and would make good their shortcomings in other areas, through exchange.

David Yates, in his Thames valley case-study, has suggested that the groups of more intensive livestock farms in the valley floor would have obtained their supplies of cereals from the uplands outside the valley. I think something similar happened at Fengate. One additional factor in the switch to mixed farming may have been the widespread introduction of breadwheat in the form of Spelt, or *Triticum spelta*. Recent research, however, indicates that Spelt was in use in Britain during the Late Bronze Age; indeed a small Late Bronze Age pit excavated in Fengate recently produced several grains and chaff fragments of Spelt.

So, to sum up, it would seem that, taken together, the change from intensive livestock to a more mixed style of farming in the mid-first millennium BC was due to a combination of factors: the ready availability of new crops, wetter ground conditions and less reliable summer grazing, coupled with a growing population and other, purely social influences that were stirring in Britain, as elsewhere in Europe. Sadly these are beyond the scope of this book.

A Bronze Age bonanza?

I have suggested that there was a millennium or so of intensive livestock farming in large parts of lowland Britain. Where we have been able to examine the ancient landscapes closely, we have found clear evidence that things were stirring well before the start of the Bronze Age. I suggest that the reason the fields suddenly appear, fully formed as it were, may be due to two factors. First, that later bank maintenance and ditch cleaning removed most traces of earlier activity and, second, that sub-division of fields is extremely hard to detect archaeologically. I also think it probable that the appearance of fields came at a time when the population of animals suddenly passed a critical threshold and it then became necessary to parcel-up the landscape more formally; this would have been an all-or-nothing affair: one either parcels-up the landscape, or one doesn't. It makes no sense to carry out such work piecemeal.

The rapid dividing-up of entire landscapes would indicate that pre-existing tenurial agreements were well understood and were formalised, a view that finds support from the even or focal distribution of barrows through the later field systems. Everything argues in favour of gradual change and continuity leading to a 'climax' system which worked very well and for a long time. When such well-established systems break down, the collapse can be sudden and dramatic, and that seems to have been what happened in the early years of the Iron Age.

The period of intensive livestock farming had been most remarkable: it was a time of great prosperity and I can find no good evidence that these benefits were not enjoyed by a large proportion of society. Certainly the items dropped into the waters at Flag Fen range from quernstones, to pins, to dogs, to swords — a broad cross-section of material culture, if ever there was one. I am sure that the greedy, rich and powerful managed to grab more than their fair share, as they will always do, but at least in the Bronze Age they then offered their wealth to the waters — and thereby to us. So in a sense we are playing the role of their ancestors, and not *vice versa*. It's all rather odd.

Suggestions for further reading

As was noted in Chapter 1, this is not a text-book and it relies heavily on ideas that have accumulated in my mind over the years. Many of these thoughts doubtless came from other people and are not original, in which case I apologise — I have simply forgotten the original sources. The suggestions for further reading are not meant to be exhaustive, but rather to point the reader in the right general direction.

1 Farmers and prehistory

This is essentially a personal chapter and I hesitate to direct the reader anywhere to find out more! But I will take the opportunity to recommend the journal of the British Agricultural History Society, *The Agricultural History Review;* described as 'a journal of agricultural and rural history', it ought to appear more often on archaeological reading lists.

2 Beginnings

For the beginnings and spread of Neolithic culture through Europe:
> Whittle, A, 1985 *Problems in Neolithic Archaeology,* New Studies in Archaeology Series, Cambridge University Press
> Whittle, A, 1988 *Neolithic Europe — a survey,* Cambridge World Archaeology series, Cambridge University Press

For the spread of Indo-European languages into Europe:
> Renfrew, A C, 1987 *Archaeology and Language — the Puzzle of Indo-European Origins,* Penguin Books

3 Them and Us — expressions of identity

Although inevitably dated, and based on a pre-radiocarbon chronology, the late Professor Stuart Piggott's text-book still provides a fine overview of the range of Neolithic sites and monuments in Britain. It will remain a remarkable achievement:
> Piggott, S, 1954 *The Neolithic Cultures of the British Isles*, Cambridge University Press

For a refreshing re-examination of the Neolithic in southern England:
> Thomas, J, 1991 *Rethinking the Neolithic,* New Studies in Archaeology series, Cambridge University Press

A collection of essays giving unusual insights into Neolithic and Bronze Age culture in Britain (it includes my own paper on the earlier Neolithic landscape at Fengate) :

Kinnes, I A and Barrett, J (eds) *The Archaeology of Context in the Neolithic and Bronze Age: recent trends*, Dept. of Prehistory and Archaeology, Sheffield University

For the early Neolithic settlement of Denmark:

Madsen, T and Jensen, H J, 1982 Settlement and land-use in early Neolithic Denmark, *Analecta Praehistorica Leidensia*, **15**, 63-86

For Holland:

Louwe Kooijmans, L P, 1993 Wetland exploitation and upland relations of prehistoric communities in the Netherlands, in J Gardiner (ed), *Flatlands and Wetlands: current themes in East Anglian archaeology*, East Anglian Archaeology, No. **50**, 71-116

A good, short account of causewayed enclosures in general (with full references):

Mercer, R J, 1990 *Causewayed Enclosures,* Shire Publications

4 Maccus' Island

For Maxey and the lower Welland in general (with numerous references):

Pryor, F M M and French, C A I, 1985 *Archaeology and Environment in the lower Welland valley*, 2 vols. East Anglian Archaeology No. **27**

The definitive report on Etton:

Pryor, F M M, 1998 *Etton — excavations at a Neolithic causewayed enclosure near Maxey, Cambridgeshire, 1982-87* English Heritage Archaeological Report **18**

For Fenland archaeology (with numerous references):

Hall, D N and Coles, J M, 1994 *Fenland Survey — an essay in landscape and persistence,* English Heritage Archaeological Report **1**

5 The longevity of landscapes

For hedges, their dating and significance see:

Pollard, E, Hooper, M D and Moore, N W, 1974 *Hedges*, Collins New Naturalist Series, No. 58

6 Slicing up the landscape

For Fengate Site 11 see:

Pryor, F M M, Excavations at Site 11, Fengate, Peterborough 1969 in Simpson, WG, Gurney, D A, Neve, J and Pryor, F M M, 1993 *Excavations in Peterborough and the Lower Welland Valley 1960-69*, pp 127-40, East Anglian Archaeology No. **61**

For Fison Way, Thetford see:

Gregory, A K, 1991 *Excavations in Thetford 1980-1982, Fison Way*, 2 vols, East Anglian Archaeology No. **53**

7 Farms and fields

For more about handling and managing livestock (with references):
> Pryor, F M M, 1996 Sheep, stockyards and field systems: Bronze Age livestock populations in the Fenlands of eastern England, *Antiquity* **70**, 313-24

8 Down in the Deepings

For West Deeping:
> The site will be published in due course, but for the time being the Antiquity (**70**) reference cited immediately above is a useful source of information.

For Welland Bank:
> A paper will appear in a forthcoming issue of *Current Archaeology* (No. 160). The full report will be published by the Trust for Lincolnshire Archaeology in their monograph series.

9 Markets, marriage and memorials

For a slightly out-dated account of Flag Fen see:
> Pryor, F M M, 1991 *Flag Fen: prehistoric Fenland centre*, B T Batsford/English Heritage

10 A bridge across the Styx

For a much fuller treatment of Flag Fen and Fengate see:
> Pryor, F M M, in press *Archaeology and Environment of the Flag Fen Basin*, English Heritage Archaeological Report (completed, due out early in 1999)

11 Further afield, in space and time

For Thames valley fields see:
> Yates, D, 1998 Bronze Age field systems in the Thames valley, *Oxford Journal of Archaeology (due 1998)*

For Bronze Age metalwork in the Trent see:
> Scurfield, C J, 1997 Bronze Age metalworking from the river Trent in Nottinghamshire, Transactions of the Thoroton Society, **101**, 29-57

For the Skomer survey see:
> Evans, J G, 1990 An archaeological survey of Skomer, Dyfed, *Proceedings of the Prehistoric Society,* **56**, 247-67

Peter Reynolds' experimental farm in Hampshire was a pioneer effort to understand the practicalities of Iron Age farming; being on chalk downland it's very different to the Fens.
> Reynolds, P J, 1979 *Iron Age Farm — the Butser Experiment*, Colonnade Books, British Museum

The standard work on the British Iron Age is still:
> Cunliffe, B W, 1991 *Iron Age Communities in Britain*, 3rd Edition, Routledge, London

Index

Compiled with the assistance of Maisie Taylor
Page numbers **in bold** refer to illustrations